To All Generations

To All Generations

Clara Bernice Miller

HERALD PRESS
Scottdale, Pennsylvania
Kitchener, Ontario
1977

Library of Congress Cataloging in Publication Data

Miller, Clara Bernice.
   To all generations.

   I. Title.
PZ4.M6462To   [PS3563.I3766]   813'.5'4   77-24926
ISBN 0-8361-1825-1

To the dear
older brothers and sisters
in Christ
this book is respectfully dedicated

Author's Note

A word of explanation regarding the pronunciation of the name of Dan Brenneman's cousin and friend may be helpful. The Pennsylvania German enunciation puts a soft *i* in *Christ* as in *Chris*. So unless *Jesus* precedes *Christ*, the reference is to Christ, Dan's friend. Newer generations drop the *t* and call it *Chris*, but among the older Old Order the Pennsylvania German pronunciation is still preferred.

The word *Audnung* is used in this book as a colloquial expression for the German *Ordnung*. It refers to the collective rules and traditions of the Old Order Amish Church.

The following abbreviations are used: IMS (Iowa Mennonite School, Kalona, Iowa), EMC (Eastern Mennonite College, Harrisonburg, Virginia), and VS (Voluntary Service).

Except for historical characters all others are fictional. Any name bearing resemblance to persons living or dead is coincidental.

I want to thank and acknowledge those dear people who helped me so much in gathering background material for this book: John W. Gingerich and his sister Mary Gingerich, Leroy V. Miller, Lena A. Yoder, Art Yoder, Mary Swartzentruber, and others. Their help and consideration are deeply appreciated.

So we thy people and sheep of thy pasture
will give thee thanks for ever: we will shew
forth thy praise to all generations.
Psalm 79:13

The old man stirred and laid down his book and stared at the opposite wall with eyes that only gradually registered what he was looking at. He did not know what had roused him from the printed page; the sounds of the Home were so familiar and the routine always the same. Maybe some of the cleaning girls had talked loudly enough for him to hear and he listened for a moment. But there was no other sound to break into the sameness of the late afternoon and after a moment he ceased to listen and went back to his reading. But he had been reading ever since three o'clock and he was tired of it.

Again, he stared at the opposite wall. A bookcase took up a good share of it, filled with many volumes whose contents he knew by heart. *The Hiding Place* by Carrie ten Boom rubbed shoulders with *Cruden's Concordance* and *Halley's Bible Handbook*, while *The Christian and the Meaning of Money* was stuck between several volumes of *Reader's*

Digest Condensed Books. On the bottom shelf a stack of *U.S. News and World Reports* competed with a stack of *Time* and *Reader's Digests,* besides several piles of his denominational monthly.

The shelf was getting too full, making it unhandy for the cleaning girls to do a good job of dusting. He should sort through the magazines and the next time Helen came to see him he could send a bunch of them home with her to be burned but *Time* had a good article on the Bible that he wanted to keep, besides one wholly devoted to Watergate and he hated the thought of giving those up. That was about the only drawback about living here at the Home— there wasn't enough room to store all of the stuff one wanted to keep. And it was hard for the old to part with meaningful things. Life made one give up so many things as it was and surely when one was old one should be allowed to keep what one wanted.

It had used to aggravate Savilla—his habit of wanting to keep every magazine, every book he liked, but on the farm and even after they moved to town there had been plenty of room to store a man's accumulations, but here things had to be discarded every so often or there wouldn't be room for him.

He could have stayed in his own home after Savilla died but three weeks of being alone had driven all thought of that out of his mind. It was funny how someone as quiet as Savilla could so completely fill a house. Even if she seldom spoke in an evening, her just being there had made all the difference in the world. The house had been emptier than empty after she died and he had put in his application up here. Even then, he had needed to endure six months of silence until someone died and he could move in. It wasn't right to be glad that death had come to another person, but nevertheless, he had been glad when he was notified of a vacancy.

He had never regretted his decision. Not all Homes were

12

like this one. Many of them were justifiably regarded as anterooms to the tomb but if this one was an anteroom, at least it was a homey, pleasant anteroom. Not because of a pretty facade but because people in it genuinely seemed to care for each other. He guessed it was because each individual was regarded with the dignity as one for whom Christ died.

He certainly could not say he was lonely. His children were scattered. Alta and her husband, Jake Gunden, lived in Florida since Jake's retirement; Guy was a teacher in Indiana; Duane lived in Kansas; and only Helen, his youngest daughter, lived on a farm a few miles out of town with her big farmer husband, Vernon Yoder. But even if they didn't get to see each other often, the children wrote or called and Helen stopped by several times a week and her youngest, Judy, came in oftener than that.

But the Home was always busy with something. Sometimes it seemed to Dan that every women's church group and every club in the two-county area had adopted the residents of the Home as their project. No special day was ever overlooked as an excuse for a party. In fact, the various church groups almost vied with each other for prime holidays such as Christmas and Easter.

But the Home was the product of the community. One couldn't throw a rock on Main Street without hitting some member of one of the Amish/Mennonite groups, from the somberly clad people of the Old Order who dressed as his own mother and father had seventy-five years ago, to the most progressive middle-aged matrons running around in pantsuits accompanied by daughters in shorts. The town was a duke's mixture of horses and buggies tied at the hitching post behind the main department store, Pennsylvania Dutch spoken on the street by the plain people, and kerosine lamps at the hardware stores competing for space with the most modern of microwave ovens. It was genuine antiques at auction sales of the older plain people selling at outrageous prices because of the hated antique hunters from the city competing with the plain people who regarded the piece in question merely as a needed article of furniture. It was a growing number of tourists gaping at the Old Order who quietly went about their business and wanted only to be left alone to live out their convictions in peace. It was plain houses situated beside the most modern homes in the county—the homes of progressive Mennonites who were successful business or professional people.

It was asking for *steeper* at the bakery and having the teenage clerk know you wanted a yeast-raised coffee cake. It was telling your English-speaking grandchildren you had *laudvieg brod* and *vast* in your school lunch and their knowing it was plum-butter spread bread with pork sausage. It was churches filled on Sunday morning (even if they might not be on Sunday evening).

It was unlocked doors; it was relief sales every fall where a hand-pieced and quilted bedspread might bring over two hundred dollars just for the cause of helping others. It was telling your neighbor your grandson was going into VS and his knowing what it meant. It was a mixture of radios turned to Christian stations all day or a television program turned to sports. It was the best Sale Barn in the country and a Christian bookstore doing a good business in a town of around 2,000 people. The town was livelier than many a county seat town of greater population.

He had been in a number of communities such as this and they all seemed to be held together by the same cement. Other rural areas might lose people to larger cities and other states but here no one wanted to move away. Oh, young people might go away to college or the young men to service but, although a few went elsewhere, the bulk of them came back. This town had almost doubled in size in the past twenty years and new homes were popping up like mushrooms in the rural area around the town. Of course, the Old Order had always followed the policy of building

14

the Grandpa house in the same yard when the senior members of the family were ready to retire but now one began to hear of four generations living in the same yard. As a result land prices shot sky-high. One would think more of the younger ones would go somewhere else for cheaper land, and a few did, but most of them stayed and found a niche for living somehow. Seldom was a farm bigger than 160 acres and many of the Old Order lived on an 80-acre farm, putting the numerous children to work milking by hand or raising chickens or feeder pigs. Every acre that could be brought under cultivation had long ago been utilized and in this town there was no talk of leaving swamps for wildlife or trees along a creek for ecology. Like as not the creek had been tiled and bulldozed shut any way to make room for another high-producing field of corn or hay or beans.

Those early people who first settled here had built a better foundation than they knew, or this settlement would never have endured. Certainly many communities that had shown greater promise at the beginning had faded to nothing long since, with only a few tumbled-down graves or an occasional Yoder or Brenneman to testify to the fact that the plain people had ever been there.

He wondered what Daniel P. Guengerich and William Wertz would say now if they saw this prosperous community—they who had been so discouraged with the new fledgling settlement that they would have moved back East to rejoin their kin if they had not been too poor to do so. How were they to know that a hundred years after their first worship service, held in the crude log home of Daniel P., almost a dozen Mennonite congregations would be meeting in large buildings beside the half-a-dozen Old Order groups who still met in homes and the various splits and factions that identified with no denomination?

All of this was a part of Dan, and he and all of the others were the product of all that had gone before—good or bad.

It was comforting to know of the host of God-fearing people who had worked and worried, read the Bibles, and fought or stuck together like burrs according to how their convictions led them. It was like a solid rock foundation to know his forefathers had left their homes in the Old Country to come to America where they were left in peace to practice believer's baptism and separation of church and state. Even their refusal to participate in war had been recognized, not always with good grace but at least allowed and tolerated.

But he would be the last to say that everything was good. Because of their hard work and thrifty living it was inevitable that prosperity should come and that, coupled with the general rise of the economy since the Second World War, had brought a tide of affluence that was both a curse and a delight.

It reflected in every aspect of life. Materially, where as he had farmed with horses for the first twenty years of his marriage and had never owned more than one tractor, Vernon, Helen's husband, had four and then said good-naturedly that he could use another one. He and Savilla had had one car and where that couldn't take them they didn't go. Now, Helen had one car, Vernon drove a new pickup, their sons Gary and Jim each had a vehicle, and even Judy was now paying for her own Vega since she was out of college. He couldn't say that he thought it was wrong, exactly, but it surely dramatized his point.

Spiritually, life might not be as good as in earlier years. In vain church leaders were condemning affluence and returned missionaries and VS personnel were pleading for a simpler lifestyle. And the young, especially those who had never known an unsatisfied material want, were bitter in their denunciation of materialism. The Old Order had one standard answer for it all, maintaining the old ways their grandfathers had lived; without modern conveniences, and abstaining from following the styles and fashions of the world in dress.

Sometimes Dan wondered what his father would say if he could see the life of his descendants—his stern, hardworking father, who even if one could not say was stingy, yet, nevertheless, never let go of a dollar unless he had a good reason for it. What would Pa say about Helen's three bathrooms, he who had never had one? Or Vernon's four tractors or the three television sets in the house or the thousands of dollars Vernon and Helen paid in college tuition for their three children, he who had never gone beyond the fourth reader? What really would he say?

And yet Dan had never felt underprivileged when he was growing up and, as far as he knew, neither had any of his eight brothers and sisters. They had had plenty of food and sufficient clothing. The church had provided all of the social contacts they needed and spiritual guidance besides. All of them had turned out reasonably well both spiritually and materially, so he guessed they had gotten everything they needed.

In his mind's eye he saw them all gathered around the supper table that summer before Ma died. There was Pa at the head, with Ma at the right side just around the corner with little Elmer between them. His oldest sister, Lydie, was at the other end, opposite Pa, with Katie, just younger than Dan, beside her. Then Jacob, just older than he, first on the bench behind the table, then himself, then Will, next to Pa. In front were Barbara, Annie, and Susan, ranging in age from youngest to oldest, with Barbara, the youngest, closest to Ma, for help in being served from the big dishes of food. It was the only year all nine children had been at home. By the next winter Ma died of pneumonia and the winter after that Katie married and Jacob came of age and went to Michigan.

How few of them were left now! Lydia, Jacob, Annie, and Barbara had all died before they were fifty and Will and Katie within the past five years. Now only Susan and Elmer remained to reminisce with him about the old days.

17

Not only were few of his own family alive anymore, but so many of his old friends and acquaintances were gone. Why the Lord had seen fit to let him see his eighty-sixth year when many better ones had been taken he did not know. It was strange that so many of his own family had died before their fiftieth year and he was still hale and healthy in his eighties, having not even had a cold for years. Only a hip that gave him trouble when the weather changed and made a cane a welcome companion at times.

To be sure, a few of his old friends and relatives were here in this same Home. Old John Schlabach was down one hall three doors; they had grown up together but had never really spent much time together until both came here to live, and Newt Yoder's room was at the end of the cross corridor. Then down on the first floor were Mandy Swartzentruber, Veenie Kinsinger, Mary Bender, and Lydie Brenneman, his cousin John Brenneman's widow, besides a number of others he had become acquainted with in his years of living here in the community. The Home was always full, with a long list of applicants who wanted to come in. Since the administration had never discriminated against anyone because of race or religion, many of the residents were non-Mennonites. He had come to know and respect a number of these—one especially, James Griffith, a Baptist from the western part of the state. They shared the same birth date and that discovery had only been the beginning of their friendship. At least it showed that one never got too old to make new friends.

Another sound broke into his reverie. Some visitor down the hall was telling Old John Schlabach good-bye; John was hard of hearing so the speaker had to raise his voice to make John understand. Dan placed the book he had been reading on top of the latest issue of *Christianity Today* and *The Christian Reader* that were lying on the small table beside his rocking chair, both pieces of furniture that he had brought here when he came. Grasping the sides of the rocker firmly, he got to his feet. His glance fell on the nameplate fastened to the open door. "Daniel P. Brenneman," it said, although he had been Dan for as long as he could remember—probably ever since Ma quit calling him Baby, he thought with a smile.

John's visitor must have used the elevator, since he'd have needed to go past his door to use the stairs. But since John's hip did not hurt he decided to use the stairs himself. He glanced at the clock before he went through the door. It would be a good thirty minutes before they rang the supper bell and a walk around the grounds might clear the mist from his brain after an afternoon of reading. He should have been out anyway on such a beautiful day but the book had come from the Book Club in today's mail and he had become lost in it.

He met no one on the stairs, nothing unusual, since few people used them for the up-trip except visitors. But as he emerged from the enclosed stairwell he ran into Mandy Swartzentruber, whose room was opposite the door to the stairs.

"Getting hungry, Dan?" she asked. She, too, got along without a cane, and still walked erect. Her face was lined only enough to give her character and he considered her one of the best preserved and beautiful of all the women living here. Even if she had borne ten children and had been the wife of the bishop of one of the large churches in the area for over fifty years, she must have learned how to come to terms with the cares of life or she never would have retained this look of peace and dignity.

"Not especially. I thought I'd go outside for a while and work up an appetite. Wonder what we're having for supper?"

"Apples, for one thing," she smiled a bit. "I should know, because I helped peel them all morning." She held out her work-hardened hands to show the brown fruit stain.

19

"So? I guess they're real plentiful this fall. At least Helen said Sunday that their few trees are loaded, and Vernon is too busy to pick them and Gary and Jim are going to graduate school this fall and that leaves only Helen and Judy to pick them. Helen said she picked what she could reach from the stepladder and Judy, the little monkey, crawled up on some of the branches and got some more. Helen said she didn't know who'd get the ones at the top of the tree."

"Yes, apple picking's a man's job," Mandy said. "When the children were all at home Amos used to try and do it on a Saturday when the boys were home from school. My, we used to have apples all over the place! But I don't know if a single one of those trees is still standing. Paul and Ella said the trees were getting so old and I really believe they got in a bulldozer the other year and pushed them all down. Well, that's the way it is, I guess."

"I know. You can't keep time from going on and making changes, can you?" he asked.

"Isn't that the truth," she agreed, then fell into silence.

He turned and made his way through the entrance and out the door, waving his hand at the few who had already gathered in the lounge to wait for the supper bell.

Outside he stood for a moment and breathed in the crisp, October air. This had been a beautiful fall, almost outstanding enough to live on in the memory of the community as the fall to date happenings by. The Home was in the northwest corner of town, on a higher level than most of the surrounding area, and on the gentle slope toward the south the town spread out like a peaceful painting. Most of the women of Mennonite descent loved flowers and one could almost have had a fall flower festival this year, even as Pella had tulips in the spring. If a human hand had mixed those colors they would be garish, he thought, but since God had done it the vivid orange and magenta and scarlet and half-a-dozen shades of green and yellow and gold blended with white homes and gray patches of soil to make one of the most beautiful pictures he had ever seen.

The slope of the lawn at the Home came to an end at the last remaining cornfield within the city limits. It was ripe for the bin and a corn picker had been eating its way through the field that afternoon and even now was at the end of a row unloading into a waiting truck.

This side of the cornfield the lawn was bright green from the fall rains, bordered by flowers of every description. He began to stroll across it, intending to walk over and admire the roses when he caught sight of a slim girl in blue jeans and denim jacket making her way toward him from the parking lot.

"Hello, Grandpa," she called out.

"Why, Judy! Did you come to take me out to supper?"

"Not tonight, I'm sorry. Daddy sent me to town for a repair part after I came home from work. But I dropped by to say hello and find out if you'd like to go on a drive Sunday afternoon to see the leaves."

"Why, I surely would. I was just standing here looking at them a minute ago. I can't remember ever seeing them so nice before."

He looked at her lovingly. Was it because she was his youngest grandchild that she had such a special place in his heart? Certainly, he had never had such a rapport with any of the others, although he loved them and they seemed to respect him. To his eyes, she was a perfect specimen of girlhood, although others might have objected to a crooked tooth and the few freckles across the slightly beaked nose, but to him they were only well-loved features that made her Judy. There was just a suggestion of Savilla about her and perhaps that was what made her so dear.

She shook her long hair and smiled, "I saw you standing out here when I drove in."

"I thought I'd get some fresh air before supper. I should've been out this afternoon but I got a new book from

21

the Club in the mail and I got started reading that—"

"What's the name of it?"

"*Adventures in Prayer*, by Catherine Marshall."

"Is it good?"

"Oh, yes. But unless you're especially interested in prayer it might not mean much to you."

She smiled again, revealing that crooked tooth, and he felt a pang of love go through him. For a moment they stood in companionable silence, gazing at the panorama before them. From one of the cottages at the end of the grounds someone came through a back door and began walking catty-corner across the lawn toward them.

"Here comes Lizzie Miller to help serve supper. Must be about time for the bell to ring. I guess I was out here longer than I thought."

Judy turned to go. "I'll pick you up Sunday afternoon, Grandpa. About 2:30 be all right?"

"Yes. That'll give me time for a nap after dinner."

"Right. See you then."

They both turned and she began to run toward the parking lot. He watched until she was in her car and with a final wave he made his way to the front entry.

By this time Lizzie was right behind him, "Hello, Dan," she said. "Isn't this a beautiful evening?"

"Most beautiful," he agreed.

"I'll be sorry when winter comes," she said, pulling open one of the double doors.

"Oh, let's not think of that just yet. Let's enjoy what we have now."

The ringing of the supper bell drowned out her answer. She grinned as they both joined the waiting line in the corridor.

And now he was sitting in the lobby, waiting for Judy. Dinner was long since over and he'd enjoyed a little nap over the Sunday school paper. Dinner on Sunday was always interesting, since each Sunday a different crew from one of the congregations managed the kitchen so the regular help could have the day off. Then, too, every Sunday one of the churches came in to conduct worship services for all residents not able to attend outside. Today one of the ministers was from his own home church, called Timber by the local people, or even Bush by those who had a stronger Pennsylvania Dutch background, although the official name was Lower Deer Creek.

But with the weather still so warm Dan had gone out to church, hitching a ride with John Schlabach and his son and daughter-in-law, but coming back for dinner. Often Helen had him come to her place for dinner on Sunday after church but he understood that she and Vernon had been invited to Vernon's sister's home today.

A steady stream of people were coming and going through the lobby. He sat and watched them, all the while keeping an eye open for Judy. Old John sat at the other end of the sofa.

"Are you waiting for someone, Dan?" Old John asked querulously.

"My granddaughter, Judy."

"What?" Old John cupped his hand to his ear.

John was forgetful as well as hard of hearing, Dan thought as he repeated loudly, "My granddaughter, Judy," since he had told the others on the way home from services what he was doing this afternoon.

This time John caught it and nodded his head. Dan would have enjoyed visiting with John, who had a sly humor behind that wall of deafness, but it wasn't worth getting cranked up in the short time he had left, Dan thought. Judy should be here any moment.

All at once he saw her coming through the door. But she wasn't alone. A dark-haired young man followed her. Dan got up and started across the lobby toward her.

"Judy?"

"Oh, there you are," she said, catching sight of him and coming swiftly across to him, the young man following. She caught Dan's outstretched hand and covered it with both of hers. "Grandpa, I want you to meet my friend, Lonnie Miller."

And now the young man was holding out his own hand and Judy loosened his so Dan could reach out slowly and take it, all the while looking at him keenly. He liked what he saw. Dark hair, dark eyes, good-looking regular features—he bore a faint resemblance to someone.

"Whose boy are you?" Dan asked.

"Edward Miller's," the young man said.

"Son, when you get my age, even that won't mean a thing. Who was your grandfather?"

"Christian D. Miller on one side—"

"Christian D. Miller!" Now, he really did look at him, still holding his hand. So that was why there'd been a suggestion of someone—yes, now that he knew, there was the set of Christ's shoulders and the sweep of his hair from his forehead and the cinnamon brown eyes.

"Did you know him?" the young man asked respectfully.

"Know him? We were cousins who grew up closer than brothers." Dan let go of the hand.

"Why, Grandpa, how interesting!" Judy exclaimed. "That means Lonnie and I have common ancestors!"

"As does almost everyone in this community," Dan said wryly. "Don't you know most people around here have common ancestors? We're such an intermarried, mixed-together people that none of us can claim to be different from anyone else."

"Is that right?" Lonnie asked. "I know Mom and Dad have told us that we're related to almost everyone up here."

"Lonnie doesn't live around here," Judy was quick to explain. "How long have you lived in southern Iowa, Lonnie?"

"Ever since I was ten and I'm now twenty-four. Fourteen years."

"Where did you meet him, then, Judy?"

"He came up to IMS for his senior year and I was a junior. Then we met again last spring at his brother's wedding."

"You went to Eastern Mennonite College with my brother Glen's wife, didn't you? You were roommates or something, weren't you?"

They had all turned and were going toward the door, out into the glorious sunshine of a perfect fall day.

"Suitemates, I guess you'd say. She and I and six other girls all shared the same suite last year. Oh, Grandpa, isn't it a perfectly gorgeous day? Where do you want to go?"

"Can we go up to the Deer Creek area? Around Timber

Church and different parts of that neighborhood?" Dan asked. He had not been up that way for a while and this young man reminded him of it with peculiar forcefulness.

The young man was very polite and helped Judy into the car. He closed the door after Dan had crawled in beside her and then came around and got behind the wheel. For the first time Dan saw that this was not Judy's car.

"I didn't know there was a Mennonite church in southern Iowa," Dan said, after they had backed out of the parking lot and started down the street.

"There isn't one like you belong to, but there's an Amish Mennonite one, though."

"Do you attend there?" Dan looked closely at him across Judy. After all, he didn't dress like those—

"No, Mom and Dad left that church. We go to a Bible church, although they transferred their membership to the church in Des Moines and we kids joined there."

"How close are you to Des Moines?"

"About seventy-five miles. Too far to go every Sunday."

They were out on Highway 1 leading north from town and Dan decided he'd asked enough questions for now. He hated to be too nosy. Besides, the car was like all boys' cars, noisy with a loud muffler—this young generation—one hoped that by the time as many unwelcome noises had grated on their ears as they had on his they would get their fill of loud noises.

It didn't seem to bother Judy too much, since she was used to talking above noise and besides she was sitting closer. The two of them started a conversation of their own and Dan began to look at the countryside, only half-hearing them. As Judy had said, the trees were gorgeous. Here and there an especially brilliant one flamed like a torch from a farmyard. Praise the Lord! His sight was still keen. It was a beautiful country. Just rolling enough to make it interesting. The fields were a patchwork of pastures and hayfields, green from fall rains, and tawny rows of corn ready for harvest, with featherstitch borders of trees along fencerows. Farmsteads accented the patchwork like gay appliqué, especially as almost everyone along the highway sported flaming rows of petunias or marigolds or dahlias or, in many places, all of these and more. A verse from the Psalms came to him: "The pastures are clothed with flocks; the valleys also are covered over with corn; they shout for joy, they also sing." No wonder the Indians called Iowa Beautiful Land!

Now they were slowing down for the cheese factory corner. It used to be called Stringtown Eck, Dan thought humorously, but he wondered how many young people Judy's age knew that. Even the Old Order people called it the Keiss Haus Eck. Lonnie waited until several cars had zipped past and then swung around the corner, making Judy brace herself lest she swing too closely against him. Dan felt her slight body stiffen beside him.

It was almost eerie, the feeling that came over Dan as they got farther west. It was as if he were slowly drifting back in time. As they came to the first crossroad west of the cheese factory he said, "This is where the district line used to be," almost unaware that he had spoken aloud until Judy said, "What district?"

"The Deer Creek district. The other one down east was the Sharon district."

"What do you mean, districts?" Lonnie leaned over to ask.

"Why the church districts. Up here were Upper and Lower Deer Creek and down east were North and South Sharon."

"You mean you had districts where you were two different denominations? What difference would it have made? I mean, if you up here were Mennonite and down there Old Order or what?"

"Son, son, we were all the same. We were all Old Order."

"You were?" It was half question, half incredulous wonder.

27

"I know it's hard to believe when you see all of the—what is it—three, four different branches of Mennonites, now, but, yes, really we were all one," Dan assured him.

"What happened?" Lonnie asked.

"That's a long story. I don't know if I feel up to it today. I could talk about it all afternoon and still not do justice to it."

By now they had come to the four-way stop sign east of IMS and Dan said, again almost unaware he had spoken aloud, "This is where it all began."

"What began?" Judy asked, looking at him curiously.

"The settlement. The very first ones to come here—of our people, I mean—came to this area."

"How did they happen to settle for this? Because of rich soil?" Lonnie asked.

"No, because of wood and water—two essentials for the pioneers. They needed a good source of water because they had to dig wells by hand then and they needed wood for their houses and fuel. Up here on the Deer Creek there was plenty of both. And a good thing, I might say, because they didn't have much else," Dan said wryly.

"Who were they? Were any of my ancestors among them?" Lonnie asked.

Dan chuckled. "They were about all yours, one way or the other. Didn't I tell you that everyone is related up here? Anyhow, it all started in the spring of 1846 when Daniel P. Guengerich and his family, William Wertz and his family, and Daniel P's half-brother, Joseph J. Swartzentruber, who wasn't married, came here and settled right in this area."

They had come to the corner where Lower Deer Creek Church stood opposite Iowa Mennonite High School. Lonnie pulled into the church parking lot and stopped.

"If they settled up here, how did the Sharon districts start?" Judy asked.

"Not all of them stayed up here. Daniel P. Guengerich's moved down north of town by 1849 when they had their

28

first regular worship service so the area grew up together right from the start."

"Was Daniel P. Guengerich our common ancestor?" Judy asked, with a side glance at Lonnie.

"Honey, you'll have to go back farther. Daniel P. had an uncle by the name of Daniel J. and one spelled the last name Guen and the other spelled it Gin—"

"Good night!" Lonnie said.

Dan began to chuckle again, "Son, you haven't heard the half of it. When Daniel P.'s father died his mother married a Swartzentruber and that's where this Joseph came in. He was Daniel P's half-brother."

"The plot thickens," Judy said.

"Yes, and then to complicate things further, William Wertz's wife was a sister to Daniel J.—"

"Good grief!" Judy said. "No wonder you say we're all related. Didn't anyone move in who wasn't of the same family?"

"Oh, yes, but their children intermarried with the descendants of these families and so you still get the same thing."

"What made them come out here, anyway?" Lonnie asked. "Didn't they have settled communities and churches in the East? What made them come out to Iowa which was just a wilderness?"

"Well—I suppose cheap land was one reason. Then, too, they felt that the moral plane of the congregation in the East wasn't what it could have been," Dan said slowly.

There was silence for a moment. Then, "Didn't you grow up and live in this area a few years after you were married, Grandpa?" Judy asked.

"Yes, I was born and raised west of here on the north side of the road and after Savilla and I married we moved just this next place west. Your grandparents, Lonnie, lived just south of here, on the angling road."

"Yes, but you must not have lived up here—" Judy gestured westward with her hand—"after you were married. I thought Mother said you lived on the farm down toward town for forty years."

"We did. We bought that place from Savilla's father and moved down there after we had been married about five years."

"What about my grandparents? They didn't live up here long, did they? I thought they were Old Order. Not many of those live around here now."

"They moved in 1914. Soon after the telephone split. Your great-grandfather sold his farm, which was two miles west of this corner and a little north, and moved down to Lapland, so most of his children moved with him. You see, he stayed with the Old Order faction, and only a few went with that group, outside of his family. The Laplanders had a number of good strong congregations so it seemed natural for him to move down there."

"What's Lapland?" Lonnie asked.

"That's what we called the North and South Sharon districts or anything east of the district line, which was a mile east of here."

"Let's drive west past where you lived after you were married," Judy suggested and Lonnie obediently drove back on the road and started west.

"Child, it's all changed now," Dan said as they approached the farm. "The place has changed hands I don't know how many times. When Savilla and I lived here there was still a lot of timber around the buildings, but as you can see, all they have now are some big shade trees. I can't even remember that any of them were standing when we lived there. And the house has been remodeled and added on to until not much of the original is left."

Lonnie almost stopped the car and they all looked at the place, each seeing it in his own way. To Lonnie it was just another old home brought up-to-date with a picture window and aluminum siding, while Judy saw mostly the lovely yard and late summer flowers which were a riot of color. Only Dan saw it not as it was now, but as it had been the day he and Savilla moved there. The house had been less than fifteen years old then—one of those L-shaped houses abounding at that period, and Savilla had taken such good care of it in the five years they lived there that old B. J. Otto had said it was in better shape when they moved out than when they moved in.

How happy they had been! Their two oldest had been born there—Alta, who had moved to Kansas soon after her marriage, and Guy, who now lived in Indiana. And yet, the years they had lived there had been the years leading up to the telephone split and in that split he had lost his dearest friend, this young man's very grandfather. Lost him, not through death, which might have been bearable, but through an irreconcilable difference of convictions.

Suddenly, he was strangely pensive. When the two young people began talking between themselves he lapsed into silence with his own thoughts, hardly hearing the sound of their voices. He only looked in silence as they drove slowly westward another mile, past the place where he had been born and raised and saw that it had been turned into an old car graveyard.

"Did you really live here?" Lonnie asked.

"I was born and raised here. It looks worse every time I pass by. I haven't been up here for over four years; the last time it looked junky but not as bad as this."

"Did it go out of the family or are the present owners related to you?" Lonnie asked.

"No, indeed, they're not related. I couldn't imagine anyone of my nieces or nephews letting a place go to pot the way this has. No, it was sold out of the family when my brother Jacob died in the early thirties and since then it has been sold several times. I never met the present owner.".

Lonnie drove slowly on and Dan never even turned his head. Why try to resurrect memories from a setting that

31

bore no resemblance to the ones that were so clear in his mind? The place had changed too much; he couldn't see Pa walking from barn to shop to hog house to pasture gate on grounds that were littered with old cars, old tractors, and machinery, overgrown with horseweeds and cockleburs, Pa, who could not tolerate so much as a hammer out of place in the shop. If there was one thing that made his silent father voluble it was untidiness. "A place for everything and everything in its place" could well have been engraved on his tombstone, underneath the sober words, "Joseph J. Brenneman, November 27, 1845—February 25,1928," Dan thought wryly. No, he didn't even want to connect this place with his father.

"Now where do you want to go, Grandpa?" Judy asked. There was a tiny look of anxiety on her young face—had they stirred up some unwelcome ghosts coming past this place?

"Anywhere you want to, honey."

"Now, where did you say my grandfather used to live?" Lonnie asked, slowing down and preparing to stop or turn or whatever.

"Oh. Why, you should probably turn around and go back to Timber Corner and turn south. I don't know how many of those old roads are still open up here; it's been so long since I've gone around that way."

Lonnie drove to the corner and turned around and started back the way they had come. Dan looked in silence at passing scenes while Judy and Lonnie talked among themselves. At the Timber-IMS corner they turned south.

"All of this used to be real heavy timber," Dan broke out of his reverie to say. "So heavy that the road was almost covered over with the limbs of the big trees on each side. But you can see that most of them were cleared off except for the small timber on our left. After the big bulldozers came into being the heavy timber around here began to disappear."

"Did you have to clear off any in your day?" Lonnie asked.

"Some. We had to chop them down with an axe and then wait a couple years and burn out the stumps or clear them off with horses. But after we moved down on the other farm we didn't have to do that because there weren't as many trees down there."

"Now where do I turn?" Lonnie asked, braking for the next corner.

"Right. And your grandparents lived the first house past this one."

Lonnie slowly turned and headed in that direction.

"Oh, everything's changed here, too," Dan said. "I wonder if any of the original buildings are left? They only lived here about three years right after marriage. Then, like I said, they moved down to Lapland."

They all looked at the place, Judy with a small awakening spark of curiosity, Lonnie with intent interest, and Dan with almost forgotten memories crowding to be recognized. How often had he and Savilla driven the few miles over here to spend the day with Christ and Katie, or he alone had ridden over to Joetown for something and he had stopped in to chat with Christ alone!

But as he had said, everything was changed. Even the old windmill had been dismantled and taken away. Not a single building remained that had been standing in those long-ago days.

Lonnie had almost come to a stop but now he began to pick up speed and drove on past. "Now where do you want to go?" he asked.

"Why don't we cut east again at the next corner and drive past where you used to live, Grandpa?" Judy asked. "Would you like that?"

"Oh, surely," Dan said. "I haven't been past that place for a year but you'll have to turn around and go back to Joetown." So they drove down to the first corner and turned around and headed east. Again, Judy and Lonnie began a conversation of their own and Dan looked and looked. This, too, had been heavy timber when his memory first registered it. But gradually the trees had thinned until, when they came to where he and Savilla had lived for so long, his memory could recall only trees along the creek bottom, and now even those were gone. To Judy and this Lonnie the images printed on their memory now would be the ones they would project in their years to come. He laughed to himself at how different his own earliest memories and their present memories would be. He wondered what their eyes would see when they were as old as he, if the Lord tarried.

After another mile he directed them to turn south and soon they were approaching the place that had been home for so long. It had changed hands several times since they had left it. The family that lived there now bought it less than five years ago and already it had taken on their special mark of ownership. He and Savilla had always liked a white picket fence around the house and all traces of that had disappeared. The long porch along the front of the house, where they had never had time sit, had been torn off and an addition built on to the house. Everything was well cared for and he was glad to see it. He and Savilla had been happy there but none of their own children had wanted the place, so when he grew too old to farm it he had sold it to someone completely outside the family.

"You don't remember anything of this place, do you, Judy?" Dan asked.

"Gracious no, Grandpa. I think you moved off the year I was born."

"Oh, yes, I'd forgotten," Dan said.

"Is this the place?" Lonnie asked, slowing down. They were already almost past.

"Yes," Dan said. "We lived here almost forty years. Then we moved to town and I worked for the feed mill for another fifteen. Now I've been out of that for almost eight years."

"Are you that old?" Lonnie asked with a voice tinged with awe.

"Over eighty-six," Dan said.

"You must have seen a lot of changes in your lifetime," Lonnie said.

"Oh, yes, all kinds. But most of them came so gradually that I didn't think about them until afterward. But then that's life. You can't expect time to stand still."

By now they came to a corner again and Lonnie slowed down. "Where now?"

"Where else do you want to go to, Grandpa?" Judy asked.

"Oh, I don't care. Wherever you want to. Anytime you're ready to take me back to the Home I'll go."

"Oh, it's too early yet to take you back. Why, we've only been out an hour," Judy said. "Or are you ready to go back, Lonnie? What time do you have to start for your home again?"

"I thought I'd wait until after church," Lonnie said. "I didn't count on being home before midnight."

"How far do you have to go?" Dan asked.

"About a hundred and fifty miles. It's a three-hour drive."

"Do you like it down there?"

"Oh, kind of. The people are real friendly. Then, too, the farming is more relaxed. Up here everyone is working like sixty to get ahead, it seems like. Down there it's more of a cattle country and feeder calves are the main crop, besides beans. Most everyone has a cow herd, and then they do mostly grain farming. Not too many hogs. There's an awful lot of grassland and timber that isn't tillable."

"How did you happen to move down there?" Dan asked.

"I guess you'll have to ask Mom and Dad about that. Cheap land, I suppose."

He had turned at the corner south of the old home and gone straight east and Dan automatically glanced at every home they passed. This had been the road he had taken every time he went to town in the old days and he knew every inch of it, he thought. Now they were approaching the main highway leading to town and even Judy made no comment when Lonnie headed back that way.

In a few minutes they were pulling up in front of the Home and Dan got out.

"Thank you for taking me out this afternoon," he told them. "I enjoyed it real much. I haven't been up that way for a while. No, Judy," he said as she made a move to get out, "you don't have to go in with me. I can make it alone. I'm not that bad off yet. And anyhow, if I were I'd have no business going with you."

"You're sure?" she asked.

"Yes, yes. Just you stay there. But thank you again. And you, son, you surely brought back old memories. You can tell your father I used to be a real good friend of his father."

"Okay, I will."

"Good-bye," Dan said and headed toward the Home entrance. He turned when he came to the door and waved. Judy waved back as they drove slowly to the street.

Dan turned off the radio on his small table and picked up his Bible and sat holding it for a moment without reading. Breakfast had been over for an hour; he'd had his morning walk around the grounds which he took every day unless he was sick, he'd heard his favorite gospel broadcast, and now he was ready for his own private Bible reading.

But for some reason he could not get that boy, or young man, of Judy's out of his mind. It was remarkable how much he resembled his grandfather, Christian J. Miller. The same dark brown, wavy hair, the same reddish brown eyes, the same broad shoulders.

It was many years since Christ had been his closest friend, in fact, it was over ten years since he had passed away and probably fifteen since he and Dan had had their last talk, but some unknown chemistry compounded of this young man yesterday and the drive along the long-ago familiar places made Christ as vivid to him this morning as if he were standing directly in front of him.

As he had told Lonnie yesterday, the two of them had been cousins (their mothers being sisters), and he couldn't even remember when he first become aware of Christ. He searched deeply into the past as his hand thumbed the pages of his Bible.

He seemed to see a small boy, so small he was still wearing a dress, sitting beside his mother in a new little church, so new it still smelled of raw lumber, impatiently kicking his feet against the bench in front of him while the rise and fall of a voice droned from the front of the building. He had no idea what the voice was saying, was not even aware of recognizable words, but his mother must have wanted him to listen because she reached over and tweaked his ear and frowned sternly at him. His feet stopped and he scowled fiercely at the lady's back in front of him. The sitting lasted so long! Ma was cradling a baby in her arms but she reached down into her diaper bag and dug out a cookie for him and he took it eagerly, glad for this small activity that was allowed during a solemn Sunday morning service.

While he was eating the cookie a small person on the bench in front of him, who was sitting beside the lady at whose back he had scowled, turned around and looked at him with unblinking eyes.

"Ma, Ma, Christly," he whispered urgently to his mother, grabbing her sleeve, the half-eaten cookie forgotten.

"Shh," she whispered softly in return, shaking her head.

So he settled back and gazed back solemnly at the small person ahead of him until that one's mother made him turn around and sit down.

The cookie lasted only half long enough and then it made him thirsty. But when he pushed Ma and whispered, "Wassah," she only shook her head at him again.

Finally, the long service was over and the minute it was dismissed the small person in front of him came around the bench and shyly approached him. He, too, was wearing a dress and a white lawn pinafore, same as Dan was, and as the two stood and regarded each other, smiles broke across their faces. Then once more Dan reached up and plucked at his mother's sleeve, "Ma, Christly."

"Waas? Oh, yah, da Christly," Ma said impatiently, and began talking to Christly's mother, who had turned around, too.

For another moment the two small boys stared at each other and then Dan reached out and took hold of the other's hand.

That was the first time he was consciously aware of Christ. But the two were inseparable after that. The mothers learned not to sit either on the same bench or one in front of the other, since it was impossible to keep the two youngsters quiet through worship services. Every time after the benediction was pronounced, the two small boys found each other, like steel filings drawn to a magnetic force. In warm weather they wandered outside on the grounds, hand in hand, separated only when the parents rounded them up for the ride home. In winter they sat in a corner and giggled and played unless high spirits made the temptation to run up and down the aisle too overwhelming. Such times never lasted long though, as either Ma or Pa or Christly's father or mother, who by this time emerged as Uncle George and Aunt Lydie, had a way of grabbing them just when they were having the most fun.

They started to the same grade school together, he in tow of his sister Katie and brother Jacob, and Christly behind his brother Amos. Here, too, Teacher learned it was best to place them about three seats apart, so they contented themselves with being inseparable at recess and during the noon hour.

And what a treat it was when Ma either allowed him to go home with Christly or Christly to come home with him! Then they roamed the barnyard, the pasture, the small

39

timber north of the house to their hearts content if the weather was suitable, and even sometimes if it wasn't, drinking in the sights and sounds of birds' nests, spring peepers, violets, bluebells, blackberries, acorns, birds' song, baby calves or lambs, or the crunch of snow underfoot until they came in at twilight when Ma rang the supper bell, to go to sleep behind the stove after the bounteous meal, groggy with fresh air and good food and deeply content to be together.

He remembered how he had persuaded Ma and Aunt Lydie to let Christly go to the city with them. It was in the fall of the year and summer term was over and winter term had not yet begun; fathers needed children at home to shuck corn by hand and mothers put middle-sized and big girls to work doing fall housecleaning and digging carrots and turnips for winter. That fall had been an especially beautiful one, like this one, come to think of it, and by an all-out effort, Pa had managed to get all the corn shucked by the middle of November. Winter term was still a few weeks off and Ma wanted to buy warm flannel and stout denim and covert cloth to sew warm winter clothes for her growing family which now numbered six children. The latest, Susan, had been added only in late summer.

Going to the city was a special event, one to be planned for days in advance. And not everyone in the family could go along. Since Katie had made the trip last year, she was elected to stay at home with the toddlers and the new baby and since he, Dan, had never been there he overheard with great delight that he was to go along.

All day he wandered around in a daze of anticipation. What would the city be like? He had heard scattered bits of carelessly dropped information from his elders, so he knew it was a wonderful place. But by the next morning something seemed to be missing. It took him awhile to decide what it was. Then he realized what was bothering him. Christly wasn't going along!

40

It took him another hour or so to decide that if Christly wasn't going with them he didn't want to go along either. But Ma and Pa had disciplined him well and one never approached them lightly for a serious request like this. However, as the day wore on a sense of desperation finally drove him to the kitchen where Ma was busy peeling potatoes for supper.

"Ma," he said, standing at the side of her chair and fiddling with one of the rungs along the chair back.

"Wass wit du?" she asked so sharply that he almost gave up. But he had to ask—it would be no fun if Christly didn't share the trip with him.

"Can Christly go along?" he begged in such a small voice she almost asked him to repeat.

Instead she turned from the pan of potatoes in her lap and looked at him. He raised miserable eyes to hers.

"Why do you want Christly to go along?"

He swallowed, "It won't be any fun if he doesn't."

She looked at him keenly for another moment. "We'll have to see what Pa says," she said softly. "And maybe George still needs Christly to shuck corn."

He was dizzy with relief. "Christly says he doesn't even have to help shuck corn."

"He doesn't?"

"No. Uncle George said he could stay in the house and work for Aunt Lydie so Marthie and Barbarie could help shuck corn."

"So?"

"Uh-huh. He can come because of that."

"Vell, we'll see," Ma said and with that he had to be content.

There was one more day before the Great Day. He dared not fuss too much or Pa would be quite capable of announcing he could stay at home. But Ma must have said something to him because the next day at dinner Pa said, "So, you want Christly to go along?"

Dan almost dropped his spoon. "Uh-huh," he nodded, too choked with excitement to eat.

"Will you behave yourself if I let him go along?"

"Oh, yah, Pa."

"Humm, I hope so. But you're not always to be trusted together."

"Oh, but we'll be good. I know we will."

Pa chuckled faintly. "Suppose George and Lydie won't let him go?"

Dan looked at the table and fiddled with the edge of the oilcloth. "Then I don't want to go either."

"That's what he told me, too," Ma said, a spoonful of food poised in the air.

"Well, we'll see," Pa said, but such relief flooded Dan that he was choked again.

No more was said but that afternoon Pa went to Joetown and when he came back Christly was with him. The two small boys were dizzy with excitement. But Dan remembered that Pa had said that the two of them couldn't always be trusted so he tried extra hard to behave and made sure to do the chores right and not make Pa tell him twice to do something.

Because they had to leave at five o'clock the next morning, they did as many of the morning chores as possible the evening before. They threw extra hay down for the horses, threw extra corn to the hogs, sacked the oats for the team's feed and threw it on the spring wagon for the next day, and the whole family went to bed early. Although Dan felt as excited as at Christmas and he and Christly talked in whispers and giggled until Katie came over and made them shut up, nevertheless he did go to sleep soon and all at once Ma was shaking him and Christly and telling them to get up.

It took no second bidding. He and Christly were up and dressed in their chore clothes almost before Ma was downstairs again. The chores were soon done and breakfast was hurriedly eaten while Ma told Katie how to take care of the small children. Grossmommy Brenneman was coming over after awhile to stay with Katie and the younger ones and help her do the milking that evening so Ma had all sorts of things Katie was to tell Grossmommy.

But at last they were on their way. Ma and Pa were on the front seat and Christly and Dan in the back, all wrapped up in warm blankets with heated soapstones at their feet because it was cold. Pa and Ma talked together but he and Christly paid no attention, absorbed as they were in each other. Pa was soon on the Marshalltown-Maquoketa trail and the horses settled into a swinging trot that would continue for many miles.

By the time the sun came up and brightened the countryside it was almost as if they were in a new world. For once Dan quit talking and giggling with Christly and watched everything he could see. They crossed Old Man's Creek, although he wouldn't have known what it was if Pa hadn't turned around and told them. Dan was disappointed. He had heard so much about Old Man's Creek that he'd been sure it must be terribly big, but it wasn't much larger than Deer Creek. He told Christly so and they both agreed they liked Deer Creek better.

The drive that could now be made in twenty minutes took them three hours. By eight o'clock they were crossing the bridge over the Iowa River. This stream did surpass his expectations and both he and Christly agreed that it was much more wonderful than Deer Creek.

After they crossed the river Pa guided the team to Martin's Livery while Dan and Christly and even Ma looked in wonderment at all of the houses and people along the streets, and the teams and wagons, or teams and surreys, or single horses hitched to two-wheeled carts, or even—wonder of wonders—an automobile that whisked by them, startling the horses so that old Belle would probably have reared if she had not been so tired.

Luckily they were right in front of the livery barn and Pa

43

drove inside and right up to the hitching rack in the open shed along the back.

"Whoa," Pa called to the horses. "Well, here we are, boys."

They were already half out of the enclosing blankets, but now they exploded bolt upright.

"Is this it? Is this the city? Is this the livery barn?" Dan asked breathlessly.

A suggestion of a smile was on Pa's lips and Ma chuckled outright.

"Yah, this is the livery barn and this is the city," Pa said, jumping out of the spring wagon and going forward to tie up the team. Mom crawled out more slowly and stood brushing the dust and chaff from her black shawl, her face in the black bonnet registering some of the same excitement so evident in the faces of Christly and Dan. After all, one might go to Joetown once a week and to town once a month but the city was only a once-a-year place. Plainly it was a highlight for her, too.

"Dan, give me the halter," Pa said and Dan dived to the back corner of the spring wagon and brought out the two halters and stood by to hand them up after Pa had taken off the driving bridles. Then they unhitched the horses and Dan and Christly went with Pa to water them while Ma walked slowly toward the shed which served as the office. After they had watered the horses they brought them back to the hitching rack and tied them up. They poured the oats they had brought along into the feed troughs in front of the team. With a final tug at the harness, checking to make sure the driving bridles were neatly hung over the whipsocket, Pa was ready to join Ma.

He had to go in and check with the proprietor, and then at last they were ready to go. Dan could remember all of the happenings of that wonderful day even now after more than seventy years. Mom had gone to Strubs and Yetters besides some of the other smaller stores and at noon they had all gathered at Eavers Hotel for a hearty meal, served family-style around a long table with huge dishes of potatoes and gravy and mashed turnips and beans and then for dessert several kinds of pie. The breakfast eaten that morning had disappeard so long ago that Dan and Christly felt as if they hadn't eaten for a week. When at last they were full Dan felt like the stuffed sausages looked at hog-butchering time.

After dinner Ma stayed at the hotel with the two small boys while Pa carried the packages of things already bought down to the livery stable and checked on the horses and took the soapstones into the office to warm on the stove for the trip home. While he was gone they sat in the lobby on one of the slippery leather couches and the two small boys went fast asleep. Even Ma dozed, leaning back, her shawl and bonnet spread over her lap, her white covering getting a little squashed from leaning against the top of the couch back.

But as soon as Pa came back they were awake and ready to go again. Ma wanted to stop at the new Woolworth store, the ten-cent store she called it, and Pop thought that while they were up here anyhow they might just as well go over to the museum in the Old Capitol Building.

At the ten-cent store, Pa gave each of them ten cents to spend and Dan never in all his life afterward tried harder to make a little money go further, not even through the depression when Alta first started to college. Ma became impatient with him but Pa had an air of approval as Dan carefully chose the top, the candy, and the game that totaled ten cents. Christly selected a top, some candy, and some dominoes so they would have something different to play at his house, he explained to Dan. Then Ma picked out some more sewing supplies, some stockings for the girls, and plenty of yarn to knit warm mittens and scarves. Last of all she and Pa had a whispered consultation, the result of which was that Pa took the boys to the museum up the street and across another one while Ma stayed on to shop some more. Dan knew almost at once what that meant. Christmas was coming soon. He whispered that to Christly, who nodded wisely. If Pa heard he gave no sign.

The museum was another wondrous place, with a stuffed buffalo looking so real that Dan was glad there was a glass between them. Behind the big buffalo was a smaller mama one and behind that a baby buffalo. Some nasty-looking wolves were slinking along the side of the cage and the big buffalo had his head lowered and was pawing the ground, just ready to charge. Even though Dan knew they weren't real, he stayed close to Pa, with Christly on the other side.

There was so much to see—Indian arrowheads, and broken pottery, and on and on. Coupled with all of the things he had seen since sunup, his mind was so full that by the time Pa was ready to leave Dan was not capable of assimilating one more thing.

When they stopped at the ten-cent store for Ma the packages she carried did not even register. His feet began to feel as they did when mud stuck to his overshoes. He thought they would never cover the two blocks to the livery stable, and Christly must have felt the same way, since Ma and Pa had to walk slower and slower to accommodate their lagging steps.

By the time they got to the livery barn even Ma was breathing hard and Pa no longer had a spring to his step. They piled the packages carefully in the back of the spring wagon and Ma rearranged the blankets and then went to pay the stable owner and pick up the warm soapstones while Pa and the two boys watered and hitched up the team again. When Ma returned, holding a soapstone in each hand, Pa picked up each boy in turn and swung him into the back of the wagon. Dan was so glad! He didn't even have the strength to crawl anymore.

"They've had a long day," he heard Ma say as her capable hands put the soapstone at their feet and tucked the blankets around them. Pa's low reply went unheeded as they snuggled down among the straw and blankets and cushions. The sights on the way home were just as wonderful as on the way to the city but Dan didn't care. By the time Pa drove over the bridge of the Iowa River they were fast asleep.

4

The sound of the cleaning cart outside his door brought him back to reality. A moment later a cheerful face appeared at the doorway. "Why, Dan, why aren't you outside on a nice day like this?" the owner of the face asked.

It was Fannie May Miller, one of the Old Order girls who worked here in the home. She was blowsy and not the tidiest of housekeepers but Dan liked her best of all the cleaning maids because she was always cheerful and ready to talk or listen to tales of the old days.

"I was thinking," he said. "I got me to thinking about the first time I went to the city."

"That must have been quite an adventure," Fannie May said, leaning on the handle of her dust mop.

"It was. My cousin Christly went along. I met his grandson yesterday and that got to thinking about it."

"Now who would be that be?" Fannie May was never in any hurry to begin cleaning if there was a story in the air.

"Who? The one I met yesterday? His name was Lonnie Miller. You probably wouldn't know him but you would know his father, Edward J. Miller."

"Oh, yes. But I thought they weren't living here. Where did you meet him?"

"He was with my granddaughter Judy. He went to IMS for his senior year and they got acquainted there. The two of them took me for a drive yesterday and that's where I met him."

"And his grandfather was your cousin?"

"Yes. We were the same age and from the time I can remember we were together. I was just remembering how we went to the city the first time. Of all the traveling I've done in my life, that was the most mind-expanding trip I've ever taken. Just think, I had never been more than ten miles from home until then. That trip took me twenty-five miles from home and I saw more new and strange sights then than I did when I went to Europe with Alta and Jake for Mennonite World Conference."

"Was it really that different?" Fannie May asked, wide-eyed.

"Looking back now, I would say not. But we weren't saturated and bombarded with new sights and sounds and experiences like we are now. Unknown things seemed stranger and more wonderful. Children the age I was then seldom went out of the school district. And we had no radio or television to bring the outside world in."

"Well, we don't have them either," Fannie May pointed out.

"That's true. But even your people get out far more than the most progressive did then. For instance, how old were you when you first traveled outside the state?"

"I was just a baby," Fannie May laughed. "I don't even remember. But Mom says they went to Indiana for my grandpa's funeral before I was a year old. Then I went again when I was four for my Aunt Susie's wedding."

"Well, see. I didn't leave the state until I was married. No wonder a trip to the city was something memorable."

"Fannie May, are you about done with Dan's room?" another voice broke in and they both looked toward the door to see Emma Miller, Fannie May's supervisor.

"I haven't even started yet," Fannie May laughed cheerfully. "Dan and I got to talking."

"Well, when you're done here, come over to the west corridor. We have to change that one room around."

"Okay."

They looked at each other, as Emma went on down the hall, and Fannie May grinned. "Well, Dan, how much dirt and dust have you got today?"

"Same as always."

"Good land, Dan, if you don't get rid of some of your magazines and newspapers you'll have to move into another room." Fannie May began poking the dust mop under the bed and progressed around the room.

"I know," he said guiltily. "The next time Helen comes I'm going to have to send some home with her. Just give the bookcase a lick and a promise, Fannie May. I'll start sorting those things after you're done."

"Sure." She was stooped down to get into the corner behind his rocking chair.

"I'll just put on my coat and go outside. Nice weather like this won't last."

"No, it won't. I told Mom this morning that I can't ever remember seeing such a beautiful fall." She pushed a strand of hair halfheartedly under her covering, the dust mop pointing toward the corner.

"Not since the fall of 1898. That was the fall I went to the city for the first time. Well, I'll get out of your way now."

He had taken his jacket from the closet and slipped into it while he was speaking and now he stepped out into the corridor, pushing the cleaning cart out of the way. Fannie May was right. From the window at the end of the corridor he saw that it was a beautiful day.

After dinner he sat in the lounge with some of the other men. John Schlabach sat across from him talking about the lovely fall weather with Newt Yoder. James Griffith sat between the two of them and Dan, reading the *Moody Monthly* that had come in the mail.

"Oh, we don't have weather like we used to," John was saying. "Why, I can remember the fall I was eighteen—that would have been—let me see—the fall of 1909—it snowed on the fourth of November and we didn't see the bare ground again until next April!"

"Oh, John, we did, too," Dan said.

"Huh? What's that?" John peered across at him suspiciously.

"Why we did too see bare ground that winter. That was the year Savilla and I started going together and I remember on Old Christmas we started out to visit some young people down in Lapland in the morning in the sleigh and it warmed up so much by evening that it melted all of the snow and we had to borrow a buggy to go home. I remember it embarrassed me so—I was afraid Savilla would give me the mitten, but it didn't seem to bother her. She told me afterward she thought it was one of the funniest things she'd ever heard of." He laughed at the recollection.

"Ah, that wasn't the same year," John blustered.

"Yes, it was. You and I are the same age. We were both born in 1891."

"Well, but we had a bad winter that year," John defended himself.

"Yeah, it was, John," Newt said. "But Dan's right. I was seventeen and just beginning to run with the young folks. That Old Christmas he mentioned was the first time I had a date with a girl, and it was real nice—the sun shone all day and melted most of the snow but, if I remember right, that night a storm came up and by the next morning everything was white again."

51

"That's right," Dan said. "Then the day after that storm Pa and I went to town in the bobsled and stopped by the place—it was Old Hay John's—and hung the sleigh along behind and dragged it home that way. And after that we never saw bare ground again until spring."

James Griffith had laid down his magazine. "I wonder, could that have been the time we had that terrible blizzard? When is Old Christmas?"

"January sixth," both Newt and Dan answered.

"Well, it was the beginning of January and I was a young buck—about seventeen or eighteen. I know it was beautiful the day before and Ma hung out a big wash and not everything was ready to bring in that night. Seems to me it was some old carpets and an old quilt. Anyway, that snow came along and she couldn't get to the wash line the rest of the winter to get them in."

Then they fell to reminiscing about some of the snowstorms of their memory, each one trying to top the preceding tale.

All at once Dan chuckled. "We're acting just like all old people—talking about the past. No wonder young people get tired of hearing us spout off."

"Huh?" John asked.

"I said it's no wonder young people get tired of hearing us yap about the olden days."

"Ah, they'll do the same when they're old," Newt said. "Just give my sons another twenty years and they'll be as bad as I am—if they don't drive themselves to death before that, chasing the almighty dollar."

"Or if the Lord tarries," James said.

"Huh?" John asked.

"He said if the Lord tarries," Dan said loudly.

"Hah! Wouldn't blame Him if He came right now and made an end to it all—as wicked as the world is nowadays," John said.

No telling where the conversation might have ended had

Dan not caught sight of a familiar figure through the door from the outside entry.

"Why, there's Helen," he said, half rising out of his chair, then sitting back again.

"Hello, Father," said the woman coming toward him. "How are you on this lovely day?"

She was pretty with the blond, blue-eyed, curly-haired plumpness of middle-age and had Mennonite matron written all over her. The blue eyes were her heritage from Dan and the curly hair from Savilla—Judy got her dark brown straight hair from Vernon's side of the family. She was dressed in a jacket and skirt—she could not bring herself to wear the pantsuits so many were wearing, and although her hair was cut she had it in a French roll and Dan couldn't help feeling fatherly pride in her neat appearance.

"I'm fine, Helen. We should all be outside enjoying the nice weather but would you believe we were sitting in here talking about the worst winter storms we can remember?"

"I'd believe you old cronies were talking about anything, even the Einstein theory of relativity," Helen said, "knowing you, I would."

"Well, now, it's been a long time since I even thought of that," Dan said, "much less talked about it. That reminds me, Helen, do you have room in your house for some of my old magazines?"

"Oh, Father, you old squirrel! I suppose *Time* and *U.S. News and World Report* have both sides of the Watergate controversy that you can't throw away."

"Well—yes, they do. And I have some issues of *Christianity Today* that have some real good articles on the charismatic movement that I want to keep. But Fannie May told me this morning that if I didn't get rid of some of my magazines I was going to have to move into another room."

"Didn't think that would bother her," Newt chuckled. "I thought she just dusted where it was handy anyway."

"Yes, I can take them, Father. But I'm not promising

53

they won't be stored up in the attic."

"Oh, that's all right. Just so the mice can't get to them. Why don't we go to my room and sort them out? I'm going to keep some of the main ones here."

He got up and started down the corridor toward the elevator, Helen falling into step beside him. They met several of the other residents, Veenie Kinsinger and Mandy Swartzentruber, who had been talking with Mary Bender in her room. All of them had a word of greeting and would have enjoyed talking but Dan would not allow himself to be drawn into a lengthy conversation. When at last they came to his room, Helen sat down in a chair.

"Father, why don't you sit down too? I want to catch my breath. I was washing the woodwork in the dining room and I'm tired."

"You sit down and I'll sort out these magazines and we can talk while you're resting. You shouldn't work so hard, honey."

"You sound just like Vernon," Helen said good-humoredly, "but he never has any suggestion about who's to do it if I don't."

"Couldn't Judy help you?" He had placed his footstool in front of the bookcase area and was going through the pile of magazines.

"Oh, she does some. But she doesn't have much time after a full day on her job. She did help me clean the up-stairs Saturday, though. But our ten-room house just seems about twice as big as it did when we added on the family room and the extra sewing and bathroom five years ago. I guess I'm getting old and lazy."

"You really didn't need those extra rooms, honey."

"Oh, I agree now, but at the time we felt we needed it so the children would have more room to entertain their friends and they do use it a lot for that. Judy had that nice boy out there last night watching television until they left for church. Anyhow, what did you think of him, Father?"

"He seems like a nice young man. You know he's Christian D. Miller's grandson, don't you?"

"Judy told me this morning. Weren't you distantly related or something?"

"We were first cousins and we grew up closer than brothers," he said simply, pausing for a moment with a *Time* magazine in midair. "I was just thinking this morning of how he went along the first time I went to the city with Ma and Pa. It was the first time for him, too, as far as that goes."

"Oh, really?"

"Yes, I think so. We grew up together, started to school together, joined church together, began dating together, and got married within a month of each other. And Alta and their William were born the same winter. Edward, Lonnie's father, is one of the youngest, I believe. They had twelve children, if I remember right." He had gone back to sorting magazines.

"Well, what happened? I mean, somewhere you must have drifted apart, because I can't remember your being together after I came along."

Again he paused, this time with a copy of *Christianity Today* in his hand.

"We couldn't see alike after the telephone split. His father-in-law was an Old Order bishop and after the split the whole family moved down to Lapland. After that I seldom saw him. Just enough to keep up with the main facts of his life. Then about five years before he died I talked with him for the last time down at the mill. That must have been just about the time Lonnie's parents left the Old Order, because Christ was very bitter about them.

Helen was silent for a moment and he went back to sorting magazines. "Did all of his other children stay Old Order?" she asked.

"No, only one or two of the older sons, I believe. That was what hurt him, I guess. Here he had refused to go along

55

with us for the sake of his children and in the end most of them left when they were old enough."

"Life is funny, isn't it?" Helen asked.

"Indeed, it is. It has a way of going full circle."

"It's funny how Lonnie's parents left the Old Order and are now living in a community where there isn't even a Mennonite church," Helen said.

"That's what Lonnie said, wasn't it? They don't even attend a Mennonite church, although they still have their membership in one. Christ would turn over in his grave about that."

"They send all of their children to IMS for their senior high school year. They have one of the younger children there now, a girl, I think Lonnie said."

"How interested is Judy in Lonnie?" Dan paused above his stack of sorted-out magazines. "Or didn't she say?"

"Oh, Father, I don't know. You never can tell what this younger generation is going to do. I figure both Judy and Lonnie are old enough to make up their own minds. I had hoped that Jim and Gary would settle down long before this and they're still both bachelors. Jim says he can't afford to marry until he gets his PhD and Gary wants his MA in literature first. But it's their life, I guess. The only thing, if they got married, hopefully they wouldn't bring their dirty clothes home to me to wash. Unless they get lazy wives."

He chuckled. "That might just be your lot; you'd better be glad they don't bring one of those home. You'd be worse off than you are now."

"Oh, I know it. The only thing is, sometimes I get so awfully tired this fall that I can hardly drag myself around."

He turned and looked fully at her. It was funny how he hadn't noticed until now that her face had a pinched look. And her eyes looked dull.

"Helen, you must go to the doctor," he said sharply. "Why don't you and Vernon retire? You've worked hard enough all your life."

"Oh, I will. I already made an appointment for the end of this week. I couldn't get in before then. Besides, I've got too many things to do to take off, unless it's really necessary. But Judy has been after me, too, so I finally called in. Don't worry about me. I probably just need some vitamins. As for retiring, good grief, we're ten years too young for that. Vernon's only fifty."

He gave her another searching glance and then picked up an armful of magazines. "I guess these are the ones I'll send out with you, Helen. I hate to give them up but I'll be getting some more with good articles in them."

"Give me some of them. I can carry them out to the car."

He gave her about half of the stack and she laid them on the table while she pulled on her light coat. Then they walked together to the elevator.

5

The lovely days of fall passed with almost hypnotic regularity. Everyday he was strolling around the grounds, sometimes alone, at other times with James Griffith or Newt Yoder or all three of them together. John Schlabach's arthritis improved a bit but even so he never hobbled farther than just outside the door where he would sit in the sun for a few moments and then hobble back inside again.

The roses were especially lovely and the borders of the flowerbeds were a fantasy of mums. All of the mums given to residents over the years had been carefully given their chance to grow outside and the result was perhaps the best show of mums in the county, so striking that cars began to drive slowly around the grounds just to see them.

Judy had taken him out to supper once since Lonnie had been there and she had only mentioned his name in passing in connection with their drive a few weeks before. Neither had she mentioned much about Helen's condition beyond saying that she was taking iron tablets in an effort to get her blood count up.

So Dan lived these glorious days of fall in a deep peace, knowing that life was rich with friends of the present and memories of the past and, most of all, a lively hope for the future. So what if the present was good? He was confident that life beyond the grave was even better. He and James and Newt talked often of death, knowing that in all probability it would come to claim each of them before too long. At most, five years would undoubtedly see them in their graves.

"I'm ready to go," James said simply. "Like Paul, I've fought a good fight and I've finished my course. The Lord has been very dear to me these years. It's only a step between here and eternity. One of these days the door will open and I'll step across the threshold to meet the Lord face to face."

Dan echoed a heartfelt "Amen."

One Friday morning in the middle of November he was in his room writing a letter to Alta when Fannie May came in to clean. She was bursting with excitement because at home they were getting ready to entertain the Old Order young folks of her district after Sunday school the coming Sunday.

"You mean you still have those get-togethers?" he asked.

"Why sure we do! If we can convince someone to invite the group anyway."

"We used to have them when I was young," he said. "In the winter someone down in Lapland would have one and we'd go down there or the Lapland young people would come up to the Deer Creek districts."

"Oh, you mean all of the young people of all districts would get together?"

"Oh, yes. Don't you young people?"

"Well, sure we do on special holidays, like Christmas and New Year's Day or Easter Monday and Pentecost Monday, but no, not for just after Sunday school. This is just for the young people who are in our district Sunday school."

"Oh, I see. And you're going to have it Sunday?"

"Uh-huh. Anna Sue has been wanting one this long time but Mom said she'd have to wait until the fall cleaning was done. Well, we got that done and Sunday is the last time for Sunday school this fall and Anna Sue wanted it so much. I told Mom I'd help tomorrow and we can get the food ready then, if Anna Sue does as much of the cleaning as she can. I know Mom's getting older and can't get around very well but Anna Sue does like to have the young people there sometimes You see, she's ten years younger than brother John. I guess you'd call her our little trailer," she chuckled.

"I see. And how many young folk will you have for the meal?"

"Oh, I suppose around thirty or forty."

"Good grief! And you'll cook for all of them?"

"Oh, yes. It won't be too hard. We're going to have chocolate cake and raisin cream pie for dessert, and fried chicken and gravy and Amish fried potatoes and cole slaw and carrot salad and banana cracker pudding and—"

"*Leiver Ziet*! Stop!" Dan said in mock helplessness. "You'll send them all to the doctor with acute indigestion!"

"Oh, Dan, you're funny," she giggled. "They don't have to eat everything if they don't want to, but a lot of those boys will. You just forget how young boys eat."

"Probably, although now that you mention it, I remember how my stepmother used to say we boys ate until the food was gone no matter how much she cooked."

"Well, see. You didn't even let me finish my list. We're also going to have sliced cheese and minced ham and creamed corn and pickles and jelly and bread and butter." Again she giggled.

"Now you're making fun of me. What else do you do besides eat, at your get-togethers?"

"Oh, visit, or if the weather is nice we play games like

60

Drop the Handkerchief. If we have to stay inside we sing or play games like Dollar, Dollar, or Button, Button, Who's Got the Button, or some such game."

"Does this go on all afternoon and evening?"

"Oh, not in the evening. It breaks up at suppertime and then we go on to the singings."

"Fannie May, when you get Dan's room clean, you can go down on first floor," Emma Miller said from the doorway.

"All right, I will." Fannie May gave no indication that she had not even begun cleaning his room, but as soon as Emma's footsteps faded she came in with the dust mop and began dusting under his bed.

"Dan, you're getting magazines piled up again," she chided, as she moved to the bookcase.

"Auch, I know. I thought it looked pretty bare when I sent that stack home with Helen but you're right. They're piling up again. Helen hasn't been in as often the last while. The doctor thinks she has anemia."

"Really? That's no fun. Mom had that a few years ago and she had to take iron shots and pills and eat liver and spinach. But she's better now."

"Is she? Well, I hope Helen improves, too. Wait, I'll take this letter down for the mail and then you can clean better. Now don't work too hard tomorrow and don't eat so much you get indigestion!" he warned, as he picked up his letter and started out the door.

"Oh, Dan! You're funny!" she giggled again.

There was a slide presentation of someone's trip through the Canadian Rockies that afternoon, a program put on by one of the ladies' clubs in the community so the three men did not take an afternoon stroll, although afterward Dan and James went out to get a breath of air before supper. The slides reminded Dan of the year he and Savilla traveled through Oregon and California, and James, of the numerous trips he had taken to Wyoming to visit a sister, now

61

dead, who had been a rancher's wife.

"I used to think Iowa didn't have much for scenery in my younger days," Dan said. "I guess the wild and rugged West appeals to every young man. It's only after life has been rugged to us that we appreciate the quiet and the subdued."

"It could be," James agreed. "But don't tell me that Iowa has no scenery. The first time I came to Iowa from the Sand Hills of Nebraska I thought heaven must look like Iowa. It had been so dry out home it was like my uncle used to say—you had to prime yourself to spit. I came to Council Bluffs in June and everything was so green, and the corn was doing well, and wheat was just about ripe. I thought it was the most beautiful place I had seen. I still do."

"Yes, I think so, too, now. But I didn't when I was young. Why here comes Judy!" he exclaimed, the beauties of Iowa scenery vanishing like mist before the sun as he caught sight of her coming across the parking lot.

"I'd call her one of the beauties of Iowa, too," James smiled. "What can be more beautiful than a clean-cut young Christian girl?"

"I agree. I like her anyway," he said, watching her graceful swinging approach up the cement walk.

Of course she had seen them, maybe even before they saw her. He got up and went to meet her.

"Judy, honey, it's good to see you," he said as they met. "What are you so happy about?" he asked as he noticed the radiance of her face.

"Oh, Grandpa, I'm going down to Lonnie's place tonight."

"You are! Alone? Isn't that quite a drive?"

"Oh, not that bad. Not as bad as driving to Goshen alone and I've done that. But anyway, Grandpa, he called last night and said their church is having a special anniversary event and he wondered if I wanted to go down for it."

"So?"

"So I'm going down tonight and not come back till Sunday evening. I'm all ready to leave—my supervisor let me off work about five minutes early so here I am. Wish me luck, Grandpa!"

"Why of course. I hope you have a good time and I surely pray that God will keep you safe on the road!"

"Oh, He will I'm sure. But I have to run. I just wanted you to know."

"Well, good-bye, honey. Come and tell me about it afterward."

"Oh, I will. Bye now." She gave him a quick hug and turned to go.

He watched as she ran lightly down the walk toward her car, not moving until she had driven out of the parking lot, except to give her a final wave. Then when her car had disappeared around the corner he turned and rejoined James on the bench.

"She's going to be driving over a hundred and fifty miles alone," he told James. "Let's pray that she'll have a safe trip down and back."

"Why, surely. What better time than right now?"

So the two bowed their heads and James prayed gently for God's protecting hand over this beloved granddaughter. Dan added a hearty amen at the end. Afterward they sat in silence until the buzzer called them to supper.

◦   ◦   ◦

Helen and Vernon stopped to see him Sunday afternoon. He was alarmed at the first sight of her—caught before she saw him as the two came in through the entry. Perhaps it was just the contrast between her face and her ruddy husband that made her look so pale, he thought as the two spotted him and came across the lounge toward him.

"Hello, Father," Helen said tiredly, a wan smile on her face.

"Hello, Helen." He had half risen to catch their attention and now he sat back again. "Sit down, you two," he

63

motioned to the couch beside him. "Helen, you look tired. I told you awhile back you were working too hard. Can't you slow her down, Vernon?"

"I try to," Vernon drawled. He was over six feet tall and weighed close to two hundred pounds and Helen looked like a child beside him. "But short of tying her up, I don't know how to do it. I tell her to slow down, but she won't listen."

"Oh, fiddle," she protested, learning back against the couch and propping her head on her arm. "You never tell me how to get everything done if I do quit working. Someone has to cook the meals and wash the dishes and clean the house and wash your dirty clothes and patch them and all that, besides doing the boys' and Judy's laundry."

"I'd let those boys do their own work," Vernon said. "They're their own boss. At least they don't let anyone else boss them. Let them do their own laundry. It's a good thing you're not closer to their universities. You'd probably think you had to do their cleaning for them, too."

"Well, they don't have any wives to do it for them," Helen pointed out.

"Humph!" Vernon snorted mildly. "If they had wives, the wives would need to do that stuff for them and probably have a full-time job to support them besides so they could keep on going to school."

"Now, Vernon, this is Jim's last year and Gary's going to teach next year and just take a few courses. I guess as long as they don't have a family to support they can take their time getting their education."

Vernon said nothing, and Dan got up. "Come on up to my room. This isn't very satisfactory as long as it is Sunday. We have twice as many people coming through as on an ordinary day. You can come up and lie down if you want to, Helen."

"Who said anything about lying down?" she protested as she followed him across the lounge and down the hall to the

64

elevator, Vernon following her.

"Nobody, but you look tired," he said over his shoulder. He got to the elevator first and punched the button as he waited for them to join him. In a moment the cage came down and the door opened, discharging John and Newt. Of course, they had to stop and exchange greetings and Dan had to shout and repeat things to John, who was in one of his worst hard-of-hearing moods. It was a relief to get away at last.

By the time they reached his room Helen was really dragging.

"Helen, you must go to the doctor!" he said, his concern making him sharp.

"Father, I've been to the doctor twice in the last month," she said, sinking into a chair.

"What does he say?" Dan asked, motioning Vernon to another chair while he sat down in his own rocker.

"He gave me iron pills and told me to quit working so hard—same as all you men say who don't know what you're talking about."

"Has it made you feel better?"

She shook her head. Then he turned to Vernon, "Have you gone with her anytime?"

"No," Vernon said. "Maybe I should have but she didn't ask me to and besides, I was busy with harvest. I've got that all done now so I don't have that excuse. Helen, why don't we go see the doctor tomorrow? Maybe if I go with you and throw my weight around you'll get some results."

"I don't care." She was sitting with her head against the back of the chair, her eyes closed. Once again he had an uneasy feeling as he saw the hollow look of her eyes.

The three were silent for a moment and then she roused herself. "Judy stopped in the other evening, didn't she? She said she was going to."

"Yes, she did. Did you hear from her since she left?"

"She called after she got there. She said everything was

65

fine. She had an uneventful trip, I guess. She sounded real pleased."

"This is beginning to look serious," Dan said.

"It just might be," Helen agreed. "You wouldn't have anything against it, would you, Father?"

"No, I guess not. It's just ironic, that's all. The last time Lonnie's grandfather talked to me he was unhappy and bitter about us 'fallen away Mennonites,' as he called us who had parted from the Old Order. And now his grandson is dating my granddaughter."

"He seems like a nice boy," Vernon said. "At least he likes to farm. Maybe he'd take over our farm if none of our boys want to."

"That's silly," Helen protested. "Who says anything is going to come of it? They've only had a few dates and written a few letters to each other."

"I thought that was enough for mothers to start planning the wedding," Vernon said.

"Not this one," Helen said. "I've been disappointed too often. I don't know how many girls Jim and Gary have dated—some real nice ones, too, and nothing ever came of it. So I'm not doing any planning on this until it's a sure thing. If it ever is."

They talked of other things until the little clock on the table showed 4:30 and Vernon stretched to his full height and said, "It's time to leave, Mother. I've got to feed the steers and check the hogs and by then it'll be time for evening services."

"Oh, I know." Helen pulled herself out of her chair. "But I'm so tired I don't know if I'll go tonight."

"Helen, please see the doctor again," Dan said, standing up. "Vernon, you go with her and make sure she gets some satisfaction."

"I think I will," Vernon said.

After a few farewell remarks Dan saw them to the elevator, and then he came slowly back to his room and sank into his chair again. He was beginning to be genuinely worried about Helen's condition. Once again her pale face with the sunken eyes rose before him. What could be wrong with her? He almost felt like going down to her doctor himself, and telling him something must be done immediately. These doctors gave you a couple of sugar pills and sent you out again and never paid serious attention until you came back the third or fourth time—if they did even then, he thought disgustedly.

He didn't go to evening services that night. Now that the weather had grown colder he would stay at the Home in the evening except for very special occasions. After supper and a desultory talk with James and Newt down in the lounge he returned to his room and went to bed. His last thought as he dropped off to sleep was of Helen's pale face.

In the morning Judy called him on the telephone before she went to work, her voice husky with happiness.

"I had a marvelous time, Grandpa," she said.

"Did you? I'm glad. You got down all right and all that?"

"Oh, yes, I told you I would. I got there about nine o'clock and we sat and talked until way late. Oh, Grandpa, everyone was so friendly and nice. They couldn't have been nicer to the president."

"Is that right? And Lonnie was the nicest of all, I expect."

"Oh, Grandpa, how did you guess?"

"That's the way things usually are. Anyhow, your voice gives you away."

"Does it? Well, I really had a wonderful time. But I've got to go now. I'll take you out for supper sometime this week and tell you all about it. Maybe tomorrow evening. Would that be all right?"

"Fine. I'll expect you then."

"Right. So long!" The receiver clicked.

He stood for a moment, staring unseeing through the window. Could this be the beginning of a really serious relationship? How would he feel about having the grandson of Christ Yoder being the husband of his beloved granddaughter? What would Christ say about it if he were still alive? He shook his head at the irony of it.

As he turned away he thought, "I didn't ask her how Helen feels this morning."

When Fannie May came in to do the cleaning she was bubbling over with news of the day before. They had had a big group; some had come from other districts and they had served over forty for dinner. They had almost run out of fried chicken; by the time she and Mom sat down to eat at three there were only wings and backs left, but luckily there had been plenty of potatoes and gravy and salads and cake so the two of them had filled up on that. Anna Sue had been the last one to fill up the table before that so she had still gotten a drumstick. In the afternoon the young people had played Telegram and Dollar, Dollar. Then they had broken up into small groups and some sang and some played Scrabble and the boys played carom ("Amish pool, my brother John calls it." Fannie May giggled) and then Mom suggested getting out Anna Sue's big 2000-piece puzzle they had given her last year for Christmas which they had never completely put together and six or eight boys and girls worked on that and got it about half done before it was time to leave.

Altogether the day had been a howling success. And if that had not been enough, that evening after singing—here Fannie May's voice held the epitome of pride and affection—Anna Sue had had her first date with one of the boys who helped put the puzzle together, and he was such a nice boy! Truly she could ask no more of life for the present!

Emma had to remind Fannie May twice to go to another

room when she was done in Dan's before she reluctantly began cleaning and even then she might have bubbled on about the crowd until the third reminder if Dan had not taken pity on Emma and left the room so Fannie May would have no one to talk to.

It was now almost Thanksgiving, he mused—Thursday in a week, to be exact. He had gone out to Helen's house most years for Thanksgiving dinner, since he had come to live in the Home but Helen had said nothing about it so far and if she felt as bad as she looked she had no business cooking a big meal. He surely hoped the doctors would find her problem so something could be done about it. Maybe he could tell James and they could pray about it, he thought.

That evening Judy stopped in just as they finished supper. He had been talking about Fannie May's account of their big gathering to Newt and John and Mandy Swartzentruber, all at his end of the table, and it had reminded them so much of the crowds of their own young days that it had been like slipping back sixty-five years or more in time. So deep were they in a story Mandy was telling that Judy had to touch his shoulder before he knew she was there.

He turned with a start. "Why, Judy! When did you come in? Did you come to take me for supper? Isn't that too bad! We're just finishing up."

"No, I couldn't make it in time for supper; I knew I wouldn't. I wanted to talk to you but when I came home from work Daddy said Mother was in the hospital—"

"Oh, no, not really?"

"Yes. The doctor sent her there this afternoon for some tests. Anyway, I got supper for Daddy and me and then I came down here. I still want to go up to see Mother so I can't stay too long."

"Why don't we go up to my room?" He pushed back from the table and stood up. "You will excuse me, I'm sure," he addressed the rest of those at the table.

"Sure," Newt said and "Of course," Mandy said. John asked, "Huh? What'd he say?"

He let Newt explain and led Judy out the door and down the hall to the elevator. "Did the doctor have any idea of anything specific?" he asked.

"Daddy didn't say. He said they were going to do all kinds of tests tomorrow."

They were in the elevator now. He pushed the second floor button and when the door opened he let her go first, then followed her to his room.

"Oh, Grandpa, I came to tell you about my trip," she said, as she plopped on his bed. "It was really great. Everyone was so friendly and nice. I went to church with Lonnie yesterday morning and then they had a potluck dinner at noon and in the afternoon they had a special program. I had to leave before the evening services but I'm sure the speaker was good—" She was almost breathless.

"So you had a good time?" he asked as he settled into his rocker.

"Oh, great!"

"How were his folks? Was his family good to you?"

"Oh, yes. They couldn't have been nicer! The whole family made me feel so at home. He still has two sisters in high school and one brother at home who is through school. And his mom and dad were so nice! And can his mother ever cook!"

He regarded her radiant face fondly. Clearly she had fallen hard. "So you thought they were all wonderful?"

"Oh, yes!"

"And Lonnie, too, I suppose?"

She was suddenly shy and refused to meet his eyes. "He is one great guy," she finally acknowledged softly.

He smiled. "I suppose between him coming up here and you going down to see him you'll keep the roads hot now."

"Oh, Grandpa! There's nothing special. We're just good friends."

71

"Well, that's what they usually say. But really, I'm glad he's such a nice young man, seeing as how he has flummoxed you."

She unfolded herself and got up. "I've got to go now, though. I want to stop at the hospital and see Mother."

"Oh, yes. Let me know as soon as the doctor knows what's wrong."

"I will." She reached over and tweaked his ear, then slung the long strap of her bag over her shoulder. "So long now. Be good," she called, as she went through the door.

"I will. You, too."

She was gone.

He remained seated, leaning back against the headrest of his old rocker that felt so comfortable that he had dropped off to sleep in it many a time. Judy tonight and Fannie May this morning—both so enthralled by "a nice boy, a great guy." Judy directly and Fannie May by proxy because of her great affection for her young sister. Didn't the Bible say something about some things being too wonderful to comprehend and wasn't the way of a man with a maid one of them? Since time began girls fell for boys and boys fell for girls, and doubtless would keep on doing so as long as time endured.

Fannie May's bubbling account this morning and Judy's radiance tonight began to blend with the merry recollections at the supper table and he slipped effortlessly back in time to his first date with a girl.

Christmas was on Friday that year. Since the day after Christmas was also regarded as a holiday by the Amish, that year there was the bonus of three days of celebration in succession. Only those whose life was filled with manual work from dawn to dusk could appreciate this rare break in routine. To a young, sixteen-year-old boy who had not yet been granted the privilege of running with the young folks it seemed a magical time of coming into manhood.

As in most of the highlights of his life, Christly figured

largely in this—a Christly who was now six feet tall and who violently hated his little boy name, either protesting the name with dark scowls or other vehement denials or going so far as to threaten to fight the boys of his own age who still called him that. Even Dan had had to be reminded firmly not to call him that anymore before he remembered.

So it was now Christ and Dan. Not since Ma had died four years before had he been Daniel to anyone (or rather the German pronunciation of the name).

Even now he could remember the desolation he felt after Ma died. But a twelve-year-old boy just on the verge of manhood hides his feelings as if life depended on it and he wondered if anyone ever comprehended his loneliness for her those first two years after her death. Sister Lydie at sixteen was old enough to go ahead as homemaker in a makeshift fashion, with Pa a stern supervisor, so the family did not suffer too much from physical needs.

But Ma had been an effective buffer between Pa and the family. He wondered now if Pa had ever shown any of the other children any visible sign of affection. Modern psychiatric interpretation would probably say that there was no chance that any of them could have a happy life, considering the bleakness of their raw pioneer life and the sudden removal of the one warm factor from their life just when it was most needed.

When two years after Ma's death Pa married Lizzie Hochsteter, one of the old maids of the community, Dan had been jealous, seeing her sitting in Ma's place at the table, or using Ma's kitchen or caring for Elmer and Barbara, Ma's little ones. But as time went on and his stepmother wisely refrained from forcing herself on them, he grew to accept her and by the time he was sixteen he could see her in Ma's place without a qualm. He couldn't even remember when he first accepted her as the buffer between Pa and the family, the same as Ma had been, but on this particular Christmas holiday it was she he approached about going to

73

the young people's get-together, rather than Pa. He had turned sixteen in September, the age when the Amish young boys considered themselves as having fully attained manhood, even if their elders didn't think so. Jacob had been going to singings and young people gatherings for over a year and was even going steady with plump little Anna Yoder, and Lydie at eighteen would be marrying in a year to Harvey Miller.

But he had been too bashful to enter the world of social activities with those mysterious creatures called girls. Had it not been that Christ was urging him, he probably would have waited to make his debut until the Easter holidays or even Pentecost. But Christ, even though six weeks younger, was more self-assured and actually bold enough to talk with girls not his sisters or cousins. At any rate, he wanted to go to the Christmas singing the next day and wanted Dan to go along.

But to ask Pa for permission was more than he had courage for. Looking back he wondered why they didn't just go without asking since plenty of boys their same age would have been going. But their upbringing, especially Dan's, would have precluded that from the very beginning. They asked their parents' permission for every undertaking, certainly one as far-reaching as one's debut into official manhood.

He and Christ talked about it every time they saw each other for a month before. Christ insisting and he demurring at first, but Christ became more and more insistent as the holidays approached. Dan finally acquiesced and then actually became eager.

At last he approached his stepmother. Pa had instructed the family to call her Ma but the name stuck in his throat so he got around that by never directly addressing her. Most of the time it wasn't necessary anyway. This time he waited until only two days before Christmas when Pa had gone to town and Lydie was upstairs and the smaller children in school. (By that time Jacob was already working away from home.)

He could still feel the trepidation that made him hesitant to approach her. Almost he gave it up. Only the knowledge that Christ would go anyway gave the impetus he needed.

Afterward, he wondered that he had hesitated. She had listened gravely, not even teasing as Ma would have done, and after he had stammered out his request, she asked how old he was. When he answered that down to the year, month, and day she promised quietly to see what Pa would say.

He never knew what she said to Pa but the next day he told Dan gruffly that if he wanted to go to the singing, he guessed that Willie and Susan and Annie could get the milking and other chores done for once without Dan's help. It was almost too good to believe.

All of Christmas Day was just a prelude to the evening. The family had dinner with Grandpa and Grandma Brenneman through the day and received a new supply of hand-knitted mittens and scarves and caps. These gifts of love from Grandma were only appetizers for the evening. And when one of Dan's gifts was the songbook *Finest of the Wheat*, the book the young people used in their singings, he felt that his preparation was complete.

They went down to Lapland for the singing, held at the Issak Helmuth home. Long before time to leave Christ was at the Brenneman place. The two had decided to go together and take Dan's horse hitched to Christ's better buggy. Even now it made him smile to remember all of the planning that had gone into that venture. They were careful not to breathe a word in front of their families. They were so secretive that even Lydie didn't know they were planning to attend until she saw them at the singing.

Like most boys at their first singing they kept to corners away from bright lamplight, preferring to stay in the kitchen and watch from the fringe. But this soon proved a disad-

75

vantage for Christ. If the new boys preferred dark corners, it seemed the new girls preferred the brightest places. The only ones out in the kitchen were the latecomers, mostly girls already going steady.

"I wish we'd be sitting in the other room," Christ muttered, under cover of the singing.

"Why?" Dan whispered back.

"We can't see anything out here," Christ answered.

"I can a little bit," Dan whispered and really he could see through the opening into the living room. Like most Amish houses in Lapland at that time, the wall between the living room and bedroom was removable. At times like weddings, funerals, worship services, or singings, it was taken out, forming one large room unobstructed by pillars. This was the main meeting room and only the overflow of latecomers was seated in the kitchen. An ordinary singing would have filled only that one main room but a special occasion like Christmas brought out every single person under the age of thirty.

That evening had been as stimulating as wine. The soft lamplight gave every girl a beautiful complexion and Dan thought he had never seen so many pretty ones. Even Lydia seemed pretty, although at home she looked just like an ordinary sister. The boys who had been going to the singings regularly looked and acted so assured, talking to the girls as if there were nothing to it, and singing the songs as if they had known them all of their lives, as some of them had. But he had never heard most of them, although a few he could remember hearing Ma sing when he was just a small boy. Pa never sang.

It would have been enough for him just to watch and listen this first time but Christ had other plans. A Lapland cousin, Emery Gingerich, a year older, invited them to come to his home overnight, letting drop the information that his sisters had already invited a bunch of girls and that a few more boys wouldn't matter. When Christ's elabborately casual questioning revealed that one of the girls was Lena Bender he could scarcely keep the excitement out of his voice. He had long had an eye on Lena.

In the end, Emery was pressed into service as a matchmaker. Christ got him into a corner out behind the corncrib and asked him to ask Lena if she would have a date with him that night. When Emery came back with an affirmative answer Christ was jubilant until he remembered that he and Dan had come together. Didn't Dan want a girl, too? Dan didn't but Christ soon changed that. Lena had a cute friend, Katie Miller, and wouldn't Emery arrange a date between her and Dan? Emery could and did and almost before Dan realized what had happened he was faced with the momentous prospect of a date.

How Judy would laugh if she knew what a date consisted of in those days, he thought humorously. A date to Judy was when a boy called and picked you up and took you to a ball game or a party or a concert or a school function and took you home afterward, maybe stopping at a restaurant or pizza parlor on the way for refreshment and talk, and he might or might not come in and visit awhile when he brought you home. But a date in his day was when a boy asked to take a girl home from a singing and then tied up his horse and came in and stayed awhile—sitting up—it was called, holding the girl in his lap on the rocking chair all the time.

For a raw boy the touch of a girl was enough to inflame the senses, let alone to hold her in his lap. Fortunately the two girls were as hesitant as he was and arrangements were made for them to go to the Gingerich home with Emery and his sisters in the bobsled and Dan and Christ followed close behind in their rig.

The two Gingerich girls, Sally and Lizzie, each had a date, Emery had a girl he had been sitting up with going on six weeks—he ended up marrying her three years later—and with Lena and Christ and Dan and Katie that made

77

five couples sitting up in the Gingerich living room. Luckily, they had plenty of rocking chairs.

He could not have been broken in at a better time or with more wholesome girls. Though their merriment was subdued because of the parents behind the bedroom door, the Gingerich girls treated everything as a good joke and Emery and the older boys were in a good mood. Lena turned out to be saucy enough to deflate Christ's inflamed ego without turning him against her. Katie was as shy as Dan at first but under the influence of hilarity she was soon asking riddles and giving answers to others with the rest of the girls.

When Father Gingerich finally rapped smartly on the bedroom door to signify that he had had enough, Dan was almost as reluctant to go to bed as Christ. Emery shared the extra bed in his room with them and the three of them lay for a long time talking in low tones—all about horses and the best buggies and other boys and most wonderful of all—girls.

The next day they all went to the get-together at Dave Yoders. He couldn't remember quite as much about that day. Only that there were an awful lot of Lapland young people that he had never seen before, especially the Kinsingers and the Stutzmans and the Christner boys from around Sharon Center. He never did know the North Sharon young people as well as he did the South Sharon ones, perhaps because Savilla had been a South Sharon girl and he had associated more with those because of her.

But Savilla had not even been with the young people that first Christmas, not being considered old enough. And he had never again dated Katie, although Christ had continued sitting up with Lena for a while until she gave him the mitten (the popular saying for turning him down), and Christ turned to other girls.

Ah, those were the days! And yet, he would not go back even if it were possible. What profit would there be in returning to youth's uncertainties, the desperate groping for identity, for answers to the meaning of life? No, he had no regrets about being in the high eighties. Rather he felt sorry for Judy and her peers who still had all of those struggles to go through.

He heard someone closing a door down the hall and came back to the present slowly. The clock on his small table said a quarter to nine and he bent down to unfasten his shoelaces. It was time to go to bed—he wondered that the night aide had not yet come past to remind him.

Slowly he got ready for bed.

He was in his room the next day, reading the latest copy of *U.S. News and World Report,* which had come in yesterday's mail. In the back of his mind was a small nagging concern that would not go away no matter how interesting the article he was reading. How was Helen? Judy had been so preoccupied the night before with her visit to Lonnie's home that she had given no information about her mother, beyond the fact that she was in the hospital. What had the tests shown? He wished someone would call him and let him know.

Next week would be Thanksgiving Day and still some roses and mums were blooming. He had been outside to get some fresh air right after breakfast and saw that the sky was dark and lowering. The radio predicted rain before evening. He glanced through the window at the bit of highway he could see across the way. The cornfields all around the town had been picked by now, the beans combined a month ago, so he guessed the farmers were ready for whatever came. At least, Vernon said he was.

Just then he heard someone come down the hall and he glanced up to see who it was. But the steps slowed down just as they came to his door.

"Why, Vernon!" he cried, shocked at the sight of his haggard face. "What's wrong?"

"Helen—Helen—" His big son-in-law leaned against the door frame as if he could go no farther.

"What's wrong with her?" Dan cried sharply.

"The doctor says she has leukemia." Vernon's eyes were circles of desperation.

"No!" Dan cried in agony.

"All those tests they took—it showed up—"

For a moment Dan thought the big man would faint and he reached over and shoved a chair toward him. Vernon sank into it. Propping his elbows on his knees, he buried his face in his hands.

"Who told you?"

"The doctor. I just came from his office. I guess he got the results this morning when he went up to the hospital."

"Isn't there anything they can do?"

"He said not much. Transfusions. Medication for a while. But nothing really effective."

"Does she know?"

"I don't know. I can't tell her. Maybe she suspects it."

"Have you told Judy?"

"No, she went to work before I came down to the doctor."

For a moment they sat in silence, both too stunned for any more words. Faintly he heard the tinkle of silverware and thought automatically, "They're setting the table for dinner." He heard Fannie May giggle with someone down the hall and thought wildly, "Oh, don't come in here. I couldn't stand talking to you right now." As if in answer her voice faded away down the hall. He glanced through the

81

window and saw cars speeding up and down the highway the same as always.

Vernon roused himself and sat up. "I'm sorry I busted it to you like this. But when the doctor told me, all I could think of was to tell someone—I couldn't carry the load alone—"

"I'm glad you did. I wanted to know. I kept wondering all morning—"

"I'm going up to see her this afternoon. I thought maybe you'd want to go along."

"Yes, yes, I do, but how can I face her right away?"

"I feel the same way. If she doesn't suspect it by now, one look at my face will tell her the truth."

"Did the doctor set any time?"

"Not really. He said a couple of months, maybe a year if she responds to the transfusions and the medication."

Again they sat in silence. "Dear God, why can't it be me?" Dan cried silently. "I've lived my threescore and ten and then some, but Helen's not even fifty yet!"

Vernon shifted his big frame around and sat up. "I should go home and check on some sows that are farrowing and then I'll come back and pick you up and we'll go up to the hospital. Will that be all right?"

"Yes."

"That will be another hour, hour and a half."

"Anytime. I'll be ready."

Vernon got stiffly to his feet and Dan did, too. Awkwardly Vernon reached over and took his hand. "Oh, Dan, what shall I do? I can't face her!"

"I know it will be hard."

Tears were in both their eyes. Vernon loosened his hold and dug into his pocket for a hankerchief and blew his nose loudly. Then without a backward glance he left. After he had gone, Dan went back and sank heavily into his rocking chair.

It couldn't be! Surely the doctor had made things worse

82

than they really were. He remembered what Vernon had said and clutched at it. "A few months—maybe a year if she responds to transfusions and medication." Modern technology was so wonderful surely some medication had been discovered by now that took care of leukemia! Time was when nothing could have been done—when they didn't even know there was such a thing—only that someone wasted away and nothing seemed to help. He wondered how many of his relatives in years gone by had died of that disease and hadn't known what it was. Even when it was first known, there had been no hope but surely there was now. Surely something could be done. And yet he knew he was only arguing against that dread fear for his loved daughter.

"Face it," he thought, "death comes to all of us. It may well be that nothing can be done for her. But not Helen, yet!" he cried out silently. "She isn't half as old as I am; she should have long years to go." He got up and went to the window and looked out. Sparrows were hopping about on the roof of the low wing outside his window. "You look after the sparrows, Lord," he thought. "O do please look after Helen!"

When the dinner bell rang he was not hungry enough to make the effort to face anyone else. Someone would notice his absence and come checking up on him but no matter. He'd tell them he didn't feel hungry.

Sure enough, Myrna, the day RN, came up almost before dinner could have been over. "Aren't you feeling well, Dan?" she asked, walking over to where he was sitting and looking searchingly at him. She reached down and took his wrist and felt his pulse.

"I'm not hungry. No, I'm not sick. I just wasn't hungry," he explained lamely.

"You're sure?"

"Yes. I want to go to the city this afternoon to see my daughter in the hospital. But I just didn't feel like eating."

She gave him another searching glance as she let go of his wrist. He smiled feebly at her, hoping she would not pry any further. "If you should want anything, let me know," she said after a moment.

"I will," he said mechanically even as he thought, "Child, you can't give me anything now that will help."

So she left him again and he sat back in his chair and rocked gently, eyes closed. "O Lord, I'm almost ninety years old and I've seen a lot of grief and death, but it's never easy to give anyone up. It wasn't easy to give up Ma when I was twelve or Pa and Stepmother when I was nineteen or Savilla ten years ago and Jacob and Will and all of the others, and it isn't easy to give up Helen either. Must You take her now?"

It was about twelve-thirty when Vernon returned. His face did not look quite as gray as it had an hour and a half ago but it was still haggard. He waited while Dan got into his coat and hat and gloves and picked up his cane—he liked to have the comfort of that in his hand on unfamiliar ground—and then the two of them went down the hall to the elevator in silence.

In silence, also, they made the twenty-mile trip to the city. The threatened rain had become a reality, a gloomy drizzle that intensified their already downcast mood. Dan watched the windshield wiper swishing back and forth until his eyes hurt and then glanced out through the side windows as the landscape flashed by. Vernon usually drove like a driven man and today was no exception.

It took about as long to thread through the traffic to the heart of the city as it had to reach the city limits, but finally Vernon pulled into the Mercy Hospital parking lot.

"This all right?" he asked Dan. "I doubt if I can park any closer. I could drop you off at the door—"

"No, no, this is fine. I can easily walk from here. It's just around the corner."

"Well—then, this is it," Vernon said heavily. He rested

his big hands on the steering wheel for a moment. Then, "Can we pray?" he asked awkwardly. Dan nodded. They bowed their heads in silence for a moment. Then, "I can't," Vernon's voice broke, "you do, Dan."

"O God," Dan prayed, "our hearts are so heavy right now. It's hard to understand why this must come to Helen. If it were possible I would gladly take it on myself. I'm an old man and I've seen much life and Helen is still so young—but Lord, we don't know how You work Your ways. Just give us the grace to say, 'Thy will be done.' It's going to be hard to face Helen, knowing what we do. Just give us the grace to do that, too. In Jesus' name. Amen."

A half-sob escaped Vernon and he reached over and gripped Dan's hand. Then he pulled himself together.

"Well, it's got to be done sometime," he said, pulling the keys and opening the door. Dan opened the door on his side and stepped slowly onto the sidewalk, taking his cane and leaning on it as he waited for Vernon to lock the doors and join him. If ever he had felt the weight of his years it was on this dreary, drizzly day with the grim prospect before him. He felt almost as if his cane would not support him.

Since Vernon knew Helen's floor and room there was no waiting in the lobby for that information and he slowed his big steps down to Dan's pace as he led the way to the elevators. It came almost at once; they were a bit ahead of regular visiting hours so the lobby and elevators were not yet crowded with people.

She was on the second floor at the end of the corridor. Their steps sounded loud on the rubber tiled floor and it seemed to Dan that she would guess her illness just by the tread. Treads of death, he thought.

He was breathing harder when Vernon turned a corner and stopped at one of the first doors. "This is the room," Vernon said in a low voice.

Dan nodded and followed his son-in-law into the two-bed room.

She was asleep and he met Vernon's eyes almost with relief. But when they stepped farther into the room they saw that she was receiving a transfusion. Both of them glanced at the tall rack with its bottle of deep red blood and the thin line of plastic tubing that was carrying the vital life-giving fluid to a vein in her arm. Then Dan glanced at her again. She looked paler than ever and for the first time he noticed deep lines in her face.

The other bed was rumpled but empty; evidently she had a roommate. Without speaking, Vernon motioned Dan to take the chair beside the bed-table and went himself to get the one on the other side of the room, trying not to make any noise as he set it down close to the bed and then settled into it. Even after that she slept on.

It was almost like a reprieve. Since they did not want to awaken her they sat in silence and gradually they relaxed. Dan put his head back and closed his own eyes. Once when he opened them he saw that Vernon, too, had leaned back with closed eyes. "Poor man," Dan thought.

But a nurse came in to check on the transfusion and Helen slowly opened her eyes.

"Why, Father," she asked in surprise, "how did you come up?"

"Vernon brought me," he said huskily and cleared his throat.

She turned her head and met Vernon's eyes, "How long have you been here?"

"Not long, about five-ten minutes. How—How are you feeling?"

"About the same. But maybe not quite so tired. Maybe this transfusion will help."

There was an awkward silence. "Dear Lord, how do you talk to someone in her situation?" Dan prayed silently. Evidently Vernon was having the same problem.

"Is Judy able to get breakfast for you before she leaves for work?" Helen asked.

"Oh, sure. Sure. She gets up a little earlier than she would if you were home but that doesn't hurt her. She'd have to do that if she were married, anyway."

"Oh well, I know. But when I'm there, there really isn't any need for her to get up earlier." Helen defended her daughter. "But they'll surely let me go home tomorrow and then I can do it again."

"She can get breakfast even if you do come home," Vernon said gruffly. "You've been so tired all fall, re-member? Stay in bed until noon and get some—some rest—" His voice almost broke. To cover it he cleared his throat and coughed.

If she thought his actions suspicious she gave no sign of it. Instead she began to talk of other things, how the boys would be home next week for Thanksgiving vacation, how Judy would enjoy seeing Jim again—they had always been close—how the patient in the next bed was a farmer's wife from the neighboring area and knew some of the Men-nonites there. In careful cadences of voice Dan answered and made conversation, too, and after awhile even Vernon took part in it. Not once did she ask Vernon if he had talked with the doctor; neither did he ask whether she had. They skipped all around her illness so adroitly that it was obvious each of them had it uppermost in their minds.

After awhile her roommate came back and then they were even more careful to stay far away from the subject. When finally Vernon got up at three-thirty Dan was im-mensely relieved. His face felt as if it had frozen into a smil-ing mask. How good it would feel to let it reflect the heartache he really felt!

Only once through the good-byes did anyone break down and then it was Vernon again. "The doctor thinks—he thinks—you might—you could—come home tomorrow, you say?"

Of course he did, Dan felt like blabbing. "Vernon told me there was no use keeping Helen in here continually—

only for tranfusions or when she gets worse," he recalled. But Vernon stammered and skirted around that.

How much did she know or suspect? It was hard to tell. She smiled gently. "He hinted at that. I should know by tonight. If Judy comes up maybe I'll know by then. If not, I'll call you in the morning."

Vernon nodded. Then she gave her hand to Dan. "I'm so glad you came to see me, Father. This won't make you too tired, will it?"

"No, no, honey. Don't worry about me." Dan said. "It's her we're worried about," he thought. He leaned down and kissed her cheek. They weren't accustomed to displaying such affection but she didn't seem surprised. "God bless you, Helen," he whispered, and turned to go.

His eyes were wet. He didn't trust himself to speak or even look back but rather picked up his cane and hat and left the room. Vernon joined him before he had gone more than a half-dozen steps. And now as they walked down the corridor Dan felt the tears trickle down his cheeks. Since he still carried his hat in his hand he put it on his head and reached into his pocket for a handkerchief with his free hand. He wiped his eyes, clumsily drew the handkerchief across his wet cheeks, then blew his nose. He didn't look at Vernon but knew the big man was also having difficulty controlling his emotions.

They were silent all the way to the car. It was only after Vernon had unlocked it and they were both seated and he had already started the motor that Vernon laid his head down on the steering wheel and silent sobs shook his big body. Dan's eyes filled with tears which streamed down his cheeks faster than he could wipe them off, but he reached a free hand over and touched the heaving shoulder.

"What can I do? How can I take it?" Vernon's voice was raspy and muffled. "Why does God have to let this happen to her? What has she ever done to get this kind of a deal?"

"Oh, Vernon, don't let yourself get that way—"

"Yeah, but she's a good Christian woman—she's always been active in the church—she couldn't have been a better wife and mother—it isn't fair—it isn't fair!"

"Vernon!" His voice was sharp. "Death comes to all of us. Good Christians are no exception. We can't question the ways of God. Believe me, I've gone through this and I know that in the end God's ways are good. I know it's an awful shock, and if I could I would gladly take her place; I'm ready to go. But don't be bitter at God!"

Vernon's heaving shoulders gradually grew still and his harsh sobs subsided. At last he raised his head and reached into his pocket and pulled out his handkerchief and wiped his eyes and blew his nose. "Dad, please pray for me," he said as he put his handkerchief into his pocket again.

"I will. I do already."

The big man eased the car away from the curb and slowly pulled out into the stream of traffic. They said very little after that. The lowering sky was no longer spitting down rain and the wind had changed to the northwest. As they came out of the city traffic onto the highway heading toward home a few stray flakes drifted across the windshield. The landscape looked as cheerless as a sand dune; the grays and browns of soil and dead growth formed the drabbest picture of the entire year. Only some willows along Old Man's Creek showed a vivid chartreuse, adding a bit of color to the stark winter landscape.

Even the snow had quit by the time Vernon pulled into the parking lot at the Home. But as Dan stepped out of the car he heard the wind howling high in the treetops.

"It sounds as if cold weather's on the way," he said to Vernon, who had gotten out also.

"Yeah, I suppose I'd better get home to check the sows."

"You don't have to go in with me," Dan said raising his voice against the howl of the wind. He was on familiar ground so he hooked his cane on his arm and clutched his hat.

89

"You're sure?"

"Yes. I'll make it."

"Better get out of the wind. I'll let you know when Helen gets home."

"Yes, you do that."

Vernon turned and got back into the car and Dan leaned into the wind and walked toward the entrance. It wasn't quite so bad when he got into the shelter of the building but he was glad enough to push open the door and step inside the warm lounge.

He had told only the lady at the desk where he was going before he left, not wanting to face the ordeal of explaining to anyone. He was tired and heartsick already so he felt a sense of weariness when he ran into John Schlabach the very first thing.

"Dan! Where were you this afternoon? We wanted you for a game of checkers," John boomed.

Checkers! As if he could have played even if he'd stayed at home, knowing what he knew.

"I went to the city."

"Huh?"

"I went to the city."

"The city? Whatever for?"

"Helen's in the hospital. Vernon took me up to see her."

"What? Who's in the hospital?"

"Helen. My youngest daughter." Just as well announce it over the PA system, he thought. Well, at least this way everyone would know at once.

"She is? What's wrong with her?"

"She's sick." He couldn't keep this up, standing in the main lounge and shouting his heartache down the halls, so he sidestepped John and walked toward the elevator. Mandy Swartzentruber looked up as he passed her door but he only walked on with a brief nod.

Thank the dear Lord no one else wanted to use the elevator and he leaned back against the cage wall and wearily closed his eyes. He was beginning to feel faint and only then did he remember he hadn't eaten at noon. Never mind, supper would soon be served.

He had no more than gotten to his room, hung his coat in the closet, and hooked his cane over the closet door when a gentle tap came at the door. Oh dear, had John followed him up here? But when he opened the door James Griffith stood there.

"Dan, I couldn't help hearing—something is terribly wrong, isn't it?"

"Come in. How did you know?" He closed the door and faced James.

"You didn't eat at noon. Then all afternoon I had the heaviest burden on my heart for you. What is it? Tell me."

"Sit down, "Dan said tiredly and sank into his rocker as James sat down slowly on the straight chair. "Helen has leukemia."

"Oh, no!"

"Yes. The doctor told Vernon this morning. He came right up and told me—"

"That's why you couldn't eat—"

"Yes. Then we went up to see her this afternoon."

"Does she know?"

"We don't know. We couldn't bring ourselves to tell her, so if she knows it isn't because we told her."

"Did the doctor say how long?"

"A few months. Maybe a year. They're giving her blood transfusions and medication. But we don't know—"

"Dan, she's a child of God, isn't she?"

"Why, yes—"

"Oh, Dan, then leave her in the Lord's hands. You know that you can never love her as much as He does. Do you think He's not aware of your heartache?"

Slow tears began to course down Dan's cheeks again. "James, I needed that. I shouldn't even have let it hit me like this. I tried to tell Vernon something like that. Physician heal thyself, I guess."

"I know. But it was so unexpected, wasn't it?"

"Yes. And I could have accepted it if it had been me—welcomed it in fact. But she's still young—and needed more than I am. She can still work for the Lord and I'm so old. Humanly speaking, you'd think she would be spared," his voice broke.

James was sensitive enough not to say all kinds of encouraging things but only let him cry in silence for a few minutes. If Dan could have looked he would have seen that James's face was also wet. "You're tired, Dan," James said after awhile, "and you didn't eat at noon. You'll probably want to be alone right after supper—"

Dan nodded.

"Then let's pray now and tell the Lord about it."

Again Dan nodded. Then they both bowed their heads and James began to pray. "Dear God, our blessed heavenly Father. Thou that pitieth us more than any earthly father ever can, look down on our dear brother and lay Thy quieting hand on his broken heart. We can't know why this has come upon his dear daughter and we ask first of all if it can be Thy will that Thou would lay Thy healing hand on her and heal her. It was Thou who made our bodies and Thou canst renew those sick blood cells in her body if it be Thy will. Nevertheless, if it is not Thy will—if it is Thy will that she should have her home-going now, just remove all fear of death from her and make her fully ready to meet Thee. We plead this through the blood of our dear Lord Jesus Christ, who freely gave His life for our sakes. And comfort the family, dear Father. Help them also to see that their loss will be her eternal gain. And give brother Dan rest tonight, knowing that Thou lovest his dear ones more than he ever can. We ask this in Jesus' name. Amen."

"Amen!" Dan echoed fervently.

They clasped each other's hands as the supper buzzer rang through the building.

"One more thing," James said as they started to the door. "Do you want me to tell people anything about this? Or would you rather I was quiet?"

"They'll have to know sometime. If they ask you I suppose you'll have to tell them."

In the mysterious way of the grapevine it did get around. Mandy Swartzentruber met him in the hall and said softly, "I'm so sorry, Dan. I'm praying for you." Newt Yoder sat down beside him in the lounge the next day and cleared his throat several times before he said awkwardly, "I wish— I'm sorry, Dan," and then roughly, "Why couldn't it have been me? I'm an old jack that's no earthly good anymore." Even John, when they met the next time, clasped him roughly on the shoulder and boomed, "I'm sorry, Dan," for all of the residents to hear.

But since James's visit and prayer last night a peace had come to Dan's heart. All he had thought before, and Newt so aptly put into words, might be true if one looked at it from a purely earthly standpoint but he wasn't looking at it that way anymore; James had helped him gain his eternal perspective again. Helen was in God's hands; He loved her more than her earthly family ever could. Psalm 116:15

seemed graven in his heart today, "Precious in the sight of the Lord is the death of his saints." If this should be her last year on earth who could deny but that her every moment was lovingly guided by her heavenly Father, according to that verse?

But he sought the refuge of his own room in the afternoon; Fannie May had cleaned it in the morning so he would be free from interruption. He sank into his rocking chair and picking up a magazine, glanced through it and put it back on the pile. Then he reached for his Bible and laid it on his lap. But he was unable to free his thoughts from Helen's impending death.

Once again, that grim reaper was coming for one of his. But again a verse of Scripture came to mind, "O death, where is thy sting? O grave, where is thy victory?" His mind went back over all those of his own who had already gone on that journey, Ma, Pa, sisters Lydie, Annie, Barbara, Katie; and brothers, Jacob and Will. And when Savilla had died it almost seemed as if a part of him had also died.

Ma's death when he was twelve had already plunged him into a sense of desolation that he tried hard to hide but when Pa died five years later it was as if he were cut off completely from all moorings. How great had been the void in his heart! But does a seventeen-year-old boy show his feelings to the world? Absolutely not and he had been no exception. After Pa's death his stepmother could do nothing with him even though she tried. Legally he was under a guardian, as were the younger children. The court appointed his Uncle Will, but Uncle Will lived clear down in Lapland and seldom made the fifteen-mile journey to check on him. He hired out to a Catholic family to husk corn that first fall and since they had no scruples against it, hard cider, homemade wine, and even whiskey were freely circulated. Even now he shuddered when he thought how nearly he had became an alcoholic. Christ dropped in often to see him, and he too began to imbibe. Since he had no one else to cling to, he clung to Christ like a burr and the two boys were all that was obnoxious in teenage braggadocio.

If only he had known Jesus Christ in those days! But when someone presented the claims of Him at that time, Dan rejected Him. After his job at the Pratts was over he hired around in different places, finally ending up at John Benders, where his sister, Barbara, had been staying ever since his father's death. The Benders were childless and gladly took the little nine-year-old girl into their hearts and home and raised her as if she were their own, and now John was getting old and wanted someone to take over so he had approached Dan and hired him for a year.

How well he remembered that first spring! Since this home was now over twelve miles from the Pratts it was next to impossible to drop in for a friendly drink of hard cider or a glass or two of wine. There was so much work, what with plowing and harrowing and planting and choring, that he was literally working from dawn till dark. Even a young man in the first flush of his adult strength needs rest and the drink habit was not yet so firmly entrenched that he was willing to give up a half a night's rest for a glassful. Surely someone was praying for him.

Besides, the Benders were good to him and having Barbara there gave him enough of a sense of a family that a little of the desolation left him. To please Barbara and the Benders he began to attend church services again, a practice he had almost discontinued since he had begun working at the Pratts. Bishop J. F. Swartzentruber and Preachers Joseph Gingerich, David Reber, and Joe Hershberger, assisted by Deacon Gunden, fearlessly preached the gospel. But even if he no longer drank he still told his filthy stories, lies came just as freely to his lips, and he was not above petty pilfering if it suited him. Only on the outside did he begin to put on the appearance of respectability to please the Benders. Then, too, he first met Savilla that year and since her father was a more strict Laplander than most of the Deer Creek Amish were, he began to reform outwardly even more in a deliberate effort to impress her.

But still he had never made a voluntary commitment to Jesus Christ. Late that summer an outbreak of typhoid fever swept through the neighborhood and he was the second one to get it. He felt that someone was praying for him—he was so sick and had so nearly died. Several others who contracted the dreaded disease did die and only the mercy of God kept him alive. He knew that if he had died then he would not have gone to heaven.

Recovery came at last. By the time he was well enough to do a day's work corn harvest was on. Conscious of his returning strength, he was so glad to be alive, to breathe in the crisp air, to hear the wild geese honking overhead, to feel the rough ears of corn against his fingers, and to hear the *whop* as they bounced against the bang-board. For the first time since Pa died he was free of that feeling of being cut loose from all moorings. As he husked ear after ear of corn he resolved that he would quit his lying and stealing and close his ears and lips on those dirty jokes that he and Christ loved so well. Anything seemed possible in the triumph of returning health.

But he found that human strength is no match for superhuman temptations of the devil, working through weak human nature. Before his resolve was barely formed John Bender asked innocently one day if he had any idea what had become of that new bridle that John had bought just before the typhoid struck. Dan, who had taken it as his own less than a week after it had come on the place and hidden it in the bottom of his buggy boot, denied all knowledge of its whereabouts. John believed him so readily that Dan began to loathe himself more than ever before.

Life was more miserable than ever after that. Just before Christmas he managed enough courage to send Christ to ask Savilla for a date. He was almost nineteen and she was a year younger. His misery abated a little bit when she consented but she turned out to be so much more wonderful than he had even imagined that he tried harder than ever to live a respectable life. Every failure plunged him deeper into despair until he was about to break up their friendship. The multiplied miseries he suffered almost didn't make up for the pleasure of being with her.

He was interrupted in his reverie. It almost seemed as if the present were jealous of the past, he thought. Every time he indulged in those reveries something brought him back to the now.

This time it was the activities director, Pearl Novak. "Don't you want to come down and help us make Thanksgiving decorations?" she asked.

"Oh, I could, I guess."

"We need someone who's good at cutting plastic bottles. I thought you might be."

He shrewdly guessed that it was a ruse on her part, to keep him from sitting in his room and thinking of Helen. But her solicitude touched him and he decided to go along with her.

"I don't know how good I'd be, but I can come down and help, if you need it."

"Good. Please come."

"All right." He got up and started toward the door. "Shall I bring any tools along?"

"No, we have plenty. Just come and run what we have."

He followed her down the hall to the elevator. They talked of trivial things all the way down to the dining room where they did so much of their craftwork.

Once there, Pearl got the waiting people to cutting little baskets out of detergent bottles. Not nearly all of the residents joined; some of them, especially the women, had their own knitting or crocheting or embroidery or quilt-piecing to keep them busy, even more so as the Christmas season approached. Some of the men preferred playing checkers or putting together puzzles. Working at crafts seemed childish to them.

But Dan had never scorned them, partly because he was not as fond of games as say, John or Newt. But Newt was here this afternoon, as also were Mandy and James and Veenie Kinsinger and Lydie Brenneman, besides a half-dozen others. They all greeted him brightly and he had the feeling that this afternoon was Let's-Be-Cheerful-to-Dan-and-Help-Him-Bear-It-Day. But he went along with them. Bless their dear hearts, if they were in a situation like this, he would do the same.

They began to talk of the approaching Thanksgiving Day. James had another tale of a wild blizzard on the homestead in Nebraska when he was a boy, when the only meat available for Thanksgiving was a jackrabbit found trapped in a snowdrift. Newt recalled how they had always tried to finish husking corn by noon on Thanksgiving Day, when it was still done by hand. Then their mother always had a big dinner for them to celebrate. "But it wasn't turkey. Like as not it was the last of the roosters which had escaped the frying pan only because he could run the fastest and hid under the corncrib every time Mother tried to catch him earlier." And one year they got up at four o'clock in the morning and were in the fields two hours later. "It was in the waning of the moon and it was as bright at six as it was when the sun came up. We still had an acre to husk but we got it done by one o'clock all right. My, we were hungry! Mother had baked six squash pies and they were all gone that evening when we went to chore. They didn't last long with us four boys turned loose on them," Newt said with a chuckle.

Mandy remembered when she was a little girl and they had been invited to their German Lutheran neighbors and were served all kinds of strange and mysterious dishes, the worst of which was blood sausage. "Mama couldn't bring herself to eat it but Papa took a piece. He said it tasted like summer sausage."

99

Dan remembered how he had had to watch the sheep in the pasture along the creek since the fence was not in good enough condition to keep the wolves and coyotes from the flock. "That fall when I was six it was such a nice warm fall—about like this year—and Pa wanted to get the corn husked before he worked on the fence. Besides, he figured on pasturing the sheep only as long as the good weather lasted, and if need be, we could do without the fence that fall. So I had to take those sheep out every day and watch them all that fall up until Thanksgiving and, oh, how I hated that job! But Pa said I was too young to help with cornhusking; he had Jacob and Lydie help him with that—and every morning I had to chase those stupid sheep out—"

"Gracious, if you were six years old you should have been in school," Pearl broke in.

There was a chorus of amusement. "Child, we didn't have nine months of school in a row like they do now days," Mandy said.

"You didn't? What did you have?" Pearl asked in amazement.

"We had a summer term and winter term," Dan said. "Winter term didn't begin until after Thanksgiving. Everyone was needed to get the corn husked."

"Even when our children went to school we always had two weeks of cornhusking vacation," Newt said.

"Every country school did," Dan said. "It wasn't until after the Second World War that our little country schools quit have cornhusking vacation."

"That's when they began to have more corn picking machines and quit husking by hand," said Newt. "I think some of the schools down here in Lapland, where the Old Order went, kept having cornhusking vacations up until maybe only in the last ten-fifteen years."

"When schools consolidated," Veenie agreed.

All the while they had been visiting their hands had been cutting along an outline on the empty plastic detergent bot-

100

tles and now Newt held up his finished product. "Pearl, you've gone to school to learn things like this and I'm ashamed to say it, but I'm just a dumb farmer and I can't for the life of me figure out what we're making. What in the world is it?"

"An empty detergent bottle," Dan said soberly.

Pearl giggled. "Well, Dan's partly right, but it's to be a container to hold your Christmas cards. See, you put them in like this." She demonstrated with a package of Christmas decals lying in front of her. "You can decorate them with these little pretties and we'll give them to those who don't have letter holders."

"Well, I'll be! All out of an old detergent bottle."

"Newt, you're way behind," said Mandy. "You can make all kinds of things out of detergent bottles. But gracious me, Pearl, wherever did you get so many empty ones? You must have been saving ever since last year this time."

"I got my Sunday school class to start saving way last summer. It didn't take long."

"My goodness, Christmas will be here before we know it," Veenie said. "Thanksgiving next week and before you know it, Christmas."

"What're you going to do for Thanksgiving, Mandy?" asked Newt.

"Ella, my youngest girl, wants me to come to their place. What about you, Newt?"

"Ah, I guess I'll stay here. My family ain't having a dinner until Christmas."

"I'm staying, too," Veenie said quietly. They nodded, because Veenie had only one son, who lived in the East, and she was the only one of her brothers and sisters living anymore.

"What about you, Dan?" Newt asked gruffly, and then wished he hadn't.

"I don't know. Helen usually asks me but she might not be well enough to fix a big dinner. I might stay here, too."

Pearl took up the detergent bottle Newt had finished and pasted a little decal on it. "Look, everybody, this is the way it looks. Isn't it kind of cute?"

"It is for sure," Newt said. Then they began to talk of other things.

◦   ◦   ◦

Helen was released from the hospital the next day. In the evening Judy stopped at the Home and told him. As yet, he didn't know if she sensed the significance of Helen's illness, since she refrained from mentioning the dreaded name of the disease.

"How is she?" Dan asked. They were in a quiet corner of the lounge by themselves. The TV was going and a few of the residents were watching it. Dan had been, too, until Judy came in.

"She says she feels better. I made her go to bed as soon as I got home from work and I got supper for us. She was resting when I left."

"Are you just out for a drive or what? A date?"

"Oh, Grandpa, no. I came down to see a girl friend from college who's going through here. She lives in Pennsylvania and she's on her way to Nebraska for VS. She was another one of those girls who shared the suite with me the last year I was in college."

"Do you still hear from Lonnie?"

She met his eyes and looked down again. "Uh-huh. I had a letter from him today."

They shared a moment of silence. Then she got up, clutching her bag over her shoulder. She was dressed in the ever present blue jeans, with a fringed jacket. She shook her long hair behind her shoulders. "I suppose I'd better go, so I won't be too late getting home." She turned again. "Oh, by the way, Grandpa, what are you going to be doing Thanksgiving? You're coming out, aren't you?"

"I didn't know if your mother felt well enough—"

"Well, goodness gracious. I can cook a turkey, too, don't

you think? She'll be there to tell me how. Jim and Gary are coming home. One of them can run in and pick you up."

"Okay, I'll plan on it."

It was Jim who picked him up on Thanksgiving morning. He had not seen Helen's oldest since he had left for graduate work in the late summer. Jim was taller than Vernon, with Vernon's blue eyes and dark brown hair. One could not say he was handsome but many a girl would have been glad to settle for his broad-shouldered strength. So far Jim had sidestepped every attempt to snare him. It used to bother Helen but for the last year she had resigned herself to his unmarried state. It was his life, she had said.

Now he appeared in the door of Dan's room as Dan was reading the newest *Reader's Digest*. He had changed into his good clothes soon after breakfast, then read a few chapters in his Bible, wrote a letter to Alta, read an article in *Gospel Herald*, and now he sat leafing through the *Digest*, not wanting to get too involved in reading lest he would have to break off in the middle of an interesting article.

"Hello, Grandpa," Jim said. "Been waiting long?"

"Why, hello, Jim. No, I was just doing some reading. I thought you might come any minute. When did you get back?"

"Last night."

"Are you staying long?"

"Until Monday. I have a class Tuesday morning so I'll have to be back for that."

"So?" He had laid down the magazine and gone to the closet for his coat and hat, which he pulled on as they talked. Now he unhooked his cane from the closet door and walked over to Jim. "I'm ready now." ·

They walked together to the stairs where Jim had come up. Of late Dan had been using the elevator more and more, but never mind, they would be going down rather than up.

They met Newt in the corridor and Dan introduced Jim

103

to him. "Now don't you eat so much turkey you get the bellyache!" Newt warned. Dan smiled and nodded.

Jim had one of those modern cars that are the dream of all people under thirty but to Dan it was not as comfortable as the old Tin Lizzie that he and Savilla had owned for years. He told Jim so.

"Really? Boy, I'd love to have one of those old Tin Lizzies. What did you do with yours?"

"We drove her until she was junk. She was sitting out in the back part of the grove when we left the farm. I suppose she's rusted to nothing by now."

"What did you give for her when you bought her?"

"Oh, let me see. Around seven-eight hundred dollars, I think. We had to pinch for a while to save, but we paid cash. I took the horse and buggy to town and went in and bought her. The salesman drove me home and showed me how to drive. When we drove into the yard I was as proud of her as you are of this one. Maybe more so."

"Could be."

"I gave seven-eight hundred for Lizzie in 1917 and what did you give for your car? How can you afford to pay for a car when you've been going to school all this while?"

"I traded my other one in. Dad gave me that one. I've worked enough to make my payments."

So Vernon hadn't handed this one to him, at least. Dan was loyal to his grandsons but he couldn't help wondering when they were going to prove they had some grit by making their own way in the world.

"How many more years are you going to school?"

"I hope this stretch is it. I'll quit when I have my PhD."

"Yes, but what will you do when you're out of school? Will you get any good out of all of those years?"

"I can teach chemistry in any college in the United States then. I might even teach at S.U.I. if they have an opening."

All the while they had been talking they had been walking to the parking lot, getting in the car, leaving the small town behind, and driving through the countryside. Now Jim swung off the pavement onto the gravel that led to his father's farm. He had not mentioned Helen's illness and neither did Dan. He wondered if Vernon had told any of his children about the doctor's verdict.

Now they were within sight of the farm. Vernon's father had built the huge barn that was now outmoded with the coming of the big round balers and huge blue silos to store hay in. No longer needed for horses or dairy cows, Vernon had converted it into a hog and steer feeding operation with the latest equipment to take the place of the old hired hand or the help his own sons disliked giving. Two blue silos dwarfed even the barn, and another cement silo, the original that Vernon's father had put up, stood apart as if aware of its inferior quality. A glimpse told Dan that Vernon had the lot full of steers.

As they turned into the drive Dan was pleased with the clean yard, the rosebushes lining the drive, all the shrubs trimmed in a neat row between the yard and the road. Their place looked like a park when the grass was green and the flowers blooming. No wonder Helen had complained of being tired if she had done all that work!

The house was one of those square ones so beloved by Midwesterners in the twenties. Vernon and Helen had built onto it a few years ago and it looked bigger than ever. As he got out of the car Judy waved to him from one of the kitchen windows.

"Hi, Grandpa!" she called from the kitchen as he and Jim let themselves into the side entry.

"Hello, child. My that turkey smells good. Are you doing the work?"

"Sure. Mom tells me how and Gary helps me."

"He does? Where's he? When did he get here?"

"He came yesterday and he's watching TV in the living room. I told him I didn't need him for a while. Jim, hang his coat in the closet—"

"Oh, I'll get it, Jim. I know where to go and I'm not help-less yet," Dan said. "How's your mother, Judy?"

"Oh, Father, I'm pretty good," Helen answered herself from the living-room door where she had come to greet him.

"Why, Helen! I'm so glad to see you." He moved over and gave her a hug—he could not help it, even if he was normally not demonstrative.

"Oh, Father—I know—It's just that—Well, it may not always—"

So she knew. Or suspected. He felt her wet cheek on his and knew that tears were in his own eyes. But if the others suspected they said nothing.

A wiry young man projected from a chair in front of the TV. "Hi, Grampa, you old codger!"

"Why, Gary! Nice to see you again." He and Helen drifted apart and Dan walked across the room and put his hand on the shoulder of Helen's youngest boy. If old Christ could have seen him he would have thought he was seeing young Dan Brenneman all over again. Of all of Dan's descendants, none of them was so nearly a rerun of him as Gary. Short, wiry, always in a hurry, his every move was a study of motion. He walked with the steel spring grace of a banty rooster and was as quick on his feet as a cat. He had taken to growing a beard and a moustache and old Christ would have said that if you shaved off the moustache he would look exactly as Dan had looked for the first five years of his marriage.

He reached up now and grabbed Dan's hand and shook it in short, hard jerks. "Why you look younger every time I see you, Grampa. How do you do it? Tell me so I'll never get any older than you are."

"Now, young man, don't tease me. I just might take my cane to you. No, no, Gary, I'm just teasing. I couldn't even lift my cane up high enough to hit you."

"If you two kids are done squabbling you can sit down,

106

Father," said Helen. She didn't look quite as pale as she had in the hospital.

He picked out what experience had proved was the firmest one of Helen's great overstuffed chairs, sank down in it, and hooked his cane over the side. The original living room had been small and square and while judged large enough for Vernon's parents' family of eight children, had not been so judged for Helen's three. Consequently, Helen had prevailed on Vernon to take out the wall between the living and bedroom years ago, when Gary was a baby, and now the living room stretched the full length of the house along the east side. Afterward, when Judy was entering her teens, they had added the family room. Since the slope of the lawn to the east was ideal, the new addition was split level—the family room on the lower level and a sewing room for Helen and an office for Vernon and another bedroom with bath, that was now Vernon and Helen's on the upper level. The carpenter had built well and the whole structure had a pleasing sense of proportion and completeness not always found in remodeled houses. When the new addition was finished Helen also had the old dining room and kitchen remodeled, with a dishwasher and garbage disposal installed. Vernon had balked a little at the latter, wondering why six hundred hogs couldn't dispose of it, but in the end Helen won out in her gentle insistence. But since she had always worked hard maybe he felt she deserved it.

The family room had a huge, beautiful fireplace, built of stones from the foundation of an old barn back in the slough pasture. Now Jim asked, "Has anyone started a fire?"

"I'm afraid not," Helen said. "Your father's been out choring all morning and Gary has been helping Judy."

"I'll get it then," Jim said, and took the two steps down to the lower level in one easy stride.

"Goodness, Gary, turn that TV down or off or something," Helen said. "Or if you want to watch, why don't you go down to the family room?"

"It's not color, Mother, dear."

"My, my, what a hardship!" Dan said. "Why, when I was your age—"

"You were married and had half a dozen kids and you had more important things to do than watch TV at eleven-thirty on Thanksgiving morning," Gary said lightly.

"Exactly!"

"I suppose you were doing what my dear father is doing, scratching for the almighty dollar."

"Gary, that's enough of that!" Helen said quietly. "If your father didn't scratch for the almighty dollar you couldn't get money from him for all of your college education."

"Oh, sorry, Mother, dear," Gary said, but you could sense he wasn't.

"What have you been doing since you came home?" Dan turned to her. "I expect you've been going after the work like you were killing snakes—"

"No, I haven't," she said quietly. "For one thing Vernon put his foot down and for another, I really haven't felt like it. But Judy is real good in helping. She does the cleaning up in the evening when she gets off work. Of course, I have the automatic washer and dryer so washday isn't the big deal it used to be. I have very little ironing anymore, what with wash and wear fabrics. I never do have as much work in winter. It's just the outside work that keeps me busy."

"We're in the mechanical age, Grandpa," Gary said. After turning off the TV he had settled down in his chair again, sprawled out with one leg slung over the arm, jerking it up and down continually in rhythm with an inner tune heard only by himself.

"You can be glad you are, young man," Dan said tartly. "Or you'd be out there shoveling manure off of the hog floor rather than letting your dad push a button for the hog floor cleaner."

"Neat hit," Gary acknowledged.

108

"Where is your father?" Helen asked her son. "Didn't any of you boys help him chore this morning?"

"I did before I went after Grandpa," Jim said, coming up from the family room again. "I thought he was about done then. He said he wanted to check the sows and baby pigs. I though he'd be in by now."

"Here he comes," Gary shot off from the chair. "Rest in peace now, Mother, dear."

"Oh, Gary, don't be so mouthy. Are you sure Judy couldn't use you?" Jim asked. "Pour water, carve the turkey, or something?"

"Are you hungry or sick of the sight of me?" Gary grinned.

"Both!"

Vernon appeared in the dining room archway. "Hello, Dan."

"Hello, Vernon." He noticed his son-in-law cast a quick searching glance at Helen. "You get those steers fed?"

"Jim did that." He stepped aside to let Gary through to the kitchen.

"Which wasn't so hard to do, seeing you stand at the unloader and press a button," Jim said.

"I've got to clean up," Vernon said, beginning to unbutton his work shirt sleeves.

"I laid your clothes out," Helen said. "You probably want to take a shower."

"If I have time. Do I, Judy?" He turned toward the kitchen where Judy was bent over and peering into the oven.

"For what? Oh, a shower. Yes. Do you think the turkey's done, Mother?"

"Gracious, it should be. You put it in the oven at five this morning." Helen got up and came to the kitchen.

While Judy and Gary watched she took a fork and speared the brown bird and pronounced it well done. "Do you need my help, dear?"

"Not if she has me," Gary said.

"No, Mother, you go sit down," Judy said. Her face was flushed and a light mist of moisture lay on the freckles of her nose. "Jim can pour water in the glasses and set the chairs and I'll get the other things done while Gary takes care of the turkey. I don't want you doing anything today."

Vernon had disappeared into the upper level and Dan and Helen sat in the living room and waited to be called for dinner. The odors from the kitchen became more enticing until even Dan became almost impatient at the wait. But just as Vernon came down from the upper level Judy triumphantly called, "Dinner! Come and get it, everybody!"

When they were all seated, with the sliced turkey in front of Vernon and Judy, Vernon sank down on a chair for the first time all morning. Tired but triumphant, he reached over and clasped Helen's hand. He swallowed a few times as he looked at her. Then with an effort he said, "Dan, would you ask the blessing?"

"Our dear, heavenly Father," Dan began. "Thank you for the manifold bounties You have bestowed upon us. . . ."

9

It soon became all too apparent that Helen wasn't responding to her medication. In the middle of December she went into the hospital for more transfusions and new treatments. She was no longer plump; she must have lost thirty pounds in the last month, Dan thought with an ache, and her face had lost all trace of color. Her eyes were beginning to sink into her head and her condition was generally talked about in the community with hushed voices. By now even Judy knew that her illness was critical and likely to be terminal. Whether Vernon had told his sons Dan did not know. The two of them had gone back to their world of classes and professors and books after Thanksgiving and Dan rarely heard from them between their periodical short visits home. He had written his own sons soon after he had known of Helen's illness but had gotten only one terse note from Duane and a phone call from Guy. Duane was up to his ears in some new real-estate deal and didn't see the need to

111

come unless Helen died and Guy as junior high principal couldn't get away before Christmas. Since Alta's husband, Jake, hated Iowa winters it just might be possible that they would not even come back in case there should be a funeral.

The Christmas season was like a dream. Only Judy made any effort to acknowledge it, buying the tree herself and setting it up in the living room and decorating it two weeks before the holiday. Helen came back home after another week's stay at the hospital, this time to take to her bed with no attempt to be up.

Vernon was with her all he could be. It seemed to Dan that his big son-in-law had lost even more weight than Helen. His clumsy attempts at preparing a small lunch for himself and Helen at noon might have been responsible for his poor appetite, he who had been spoiled by years of her excellent cooking. Judy usually served a big meal at night when she was at home but she was casual with food, except on special occasions such as the Thanksgiving meal where she had really done an outstanding job.

It was well that they had faith in God to cling to, Dan thought. Even with that, it seemed to him that he had never gone through a trial with this peculiar pain. When Ma died it was an infant's desolation, when Pa, it was like being cut loose with no anchor. Losing Savilla had been like giving up part of himself. But standing helplessly by and watching one of his beloved children, the youngest and closest at that, waste away was like nothing else he had ever experienced. No wonder one of the country's most prominent women, after losing four of her children, had said that it was not right that parents bury their children, but rather children should bury their parents. There must be something one could do.

But there was not. Since Helen had been given so many transfusions the entire congregation was asked to donate blood if at all possible and the shocked and loyal fellowship complied gladly. Then, too, she was remembered at every

112

prayer meeting held in the community, except perhaps the church Amish. The Old Order had no prayer meetings.

Dan thought often of the verse, "Precious in the sight of the Lord is the death of his saints." He was out at Helen's side often these days. Either he caught a ride out with someone or Vernon came after him. They hated to leave her alone and he could stay with her while Vernon was choring. There were only the steers and the fat hogs to care for; he had sold the sows and pigs the week after Thanksgiving so he would have more time to spend with Helen. He could have made much more money by waiting until the pigs were weaned but for once he didn't care.

Finally, even Judy had no more hope for her mother's recovery and gave a week's notice at her job. When she told Dan that she was quitting he nodded wordlessly. "She's not going to get well, is she, Grandpa?" Judy asked and he shook his head. "Then I want to do for her what I can," Judy said. That evening she was on the telephone for an hour and by the look on her face as she came to ask him if he were ready to go back to the Home he wondered if she hadn't been talking to Lonnie.

One morning before Judy quit her job, Dan rode out to the farm with Mandy's daughter, Ella, who lived a mile beyond, and who had stopped in to see her mother that morning. Vernon waved to him briefly from the steer lot as he got out of the car. A few inches of snow covered the ground but Judy had cleared the walks and he went slowly up them and let himself in through the side door, his cane in his hand. It seemed never to be too far from his side this winter; never before had he relied on it so much—he was getting to be as bad as Newt.

The house looked clean enough; no doubt Judy had stacked and started the dishwasher before she went to work and straightened up the downstairs. Because of the padded carpeting he made very little sound as he walked through the dining room and hung his coat and hat in the closet.

113

"Is that you, Father?" Helen's thin voice called from the bedroom.

"Yes, it's me, child. I'm coming up."

He closed the closet door and went across the room to the living room and then to the steps that led to the upper level, his cane poking deeply into the carpeting as he braced himself against it going up the steps. Helen's bedroom door was at the end of the hall and he used his cane very little on his walk down to it.

It gave his heart a wrench to see her, even if he had seen her only yesterday noon. No one could look at her now and not see death on her face. But this morning her face seemed to be illuminated by a supernatural glow. "Why, Helen—" he broke off.

He had never seen a sweeter smile. "Come in, Father, and sit down. I was hoping you would come early so I could talk to you."

He sank into the chair at her bedside, his eyes never leaving her face. "Helen," he repeated.

She reached out a hand that was nothing but skin and bones and took one of his in it. "I had a most wonderful— well, I guess it was a dream—but anyway, it was so wonderful! I can't tell you—I saw the Lord Jesus and Mother and Uncle Jake and Aunt Lydie and Vernon's Mom and Dad— and—and—they were so shiny and happy! Their faces just glowed and—and they looked so young—and yet old and wise and good—and the Lord Jesus was the most wonderful of them all—and it seemed to me I had never seen anyone look at me with such love before—Oh, Father!" Her thin hand pressed his convulsively.

"Helen—Helen," he answered and reached over and took her in his arms. They cried silently for a moment, her tears wetting his coat and his staining one of the beautiful bed jackets Judy had gotten her. They pulled apart and he reached in his pocket for his handkerchief.

"I'm not going to be here very long you know," she said

114

matter-of-factly, reaching over to the bedside table for a Kleenex.

"Then you know—"

She nodded. "I had this feeling all fall of some great crisis hanging over me. Maybe that's why I put off going to the doctor so long. Then when I went into the hospital the first time and the nurses were so vague when I asked questions—and that time Vernon brought you up, I knew when I saw your faces—"

"Oh, child, and we tried to hide it from you—"

"Vernon can't hide anything from me," she smiled. "But anyway, I've known all along I would never get over this. How much time did the doctor give me?"

The unexpectedness of the question made him stammer. "A few months—maybe a year—"

"It won't be a year," she said.

They were silent for a moment. "But, Father, the last few weeks have been so precious! Way back in the beginning I wasn't ready for death. I thought I was so young and I hadn't seen any of my children marry and I wasn't a grandma yet— Oh, I had all kinds of reasons. But as time went on the dear Lord Jesus made Himself more real to me. Even though I'm sick and have lots of pain and discomfort, sometimes its as if He poured so much love over me that I can't hold it—my soul isn't big enough!" Again her voice broke and again he reached up and took her hand and covered it with his other one.

"But sometimes when I get to thinking of the children, then I can't stand the idea of leaving them. They're not ready for this. Oh, Father, what did Vernon and I do wrong?"

"What do you mean, girl?"

"Oh, I'm not saying the younger generation is going to the dogs and all that—Judy's a dear, sweet girl and I couldn't ask for a better daughter, especially since I've been sick—but the boys—they're so selfish—and Gary's so

115

cynical. He was downright nasty the time he was home for Thanksgiving."

"In what way?"

"I don't have any use for those who go around calling everyone a communist if they don't agree, but Gary's so bitter. He seems to feel Vernon and I have gypped someone because we have a home and land and some material possessions. I don't know if he thinks we should sell out and give everything away or what. I know now that we could have given more to the Lord and yet we always have given a tithe or more. It's not for me to tell what all we gave or helped others—we didn't do it to please men, we did it to help others who were less fortunate. But he seemed to want a fight with Vernon. We didn't have any peace when the two were in the house. Gary was making snide remarks against materialism all the time—and it hurt Vernon. Poor man, he's always been so generous with his family, it's a wonder we have anything at all. And then to top it all when Gary left he asked Vernon for money again. He called it a loan. If it were Jim it might be. But knowing Gary it will be a handout." Her voice was sad and soft.

"Jim isn't like that but there seems to be a selfish hardness about him—as if he'd stop at nothing to get what he wants. Father, we took the children to church and Sunday school from the time they were a month old. We supported the Lord's work all of our married life, but somewhere we failed in making Jesus Christ real to them."

He patted her hand wordlessly. What was there to say?

"The only comfort I have is in realizing that God loves them more than I ever could—that He will do all He can to draw them to Himself."

She was silent for a moment, building up her dwindling strength. Then she began again, her voice so much softer that he had to listen closely to hear it.

"If there has been one thing that I can draw strength from, it's the Bible." She looked toward it on the bedside

116

table. "And nothing has been so precious to me the last few weeks as 1 Corinthians 15, especially the last few verses." She began to quote softly, a smile of unearthly sweetness on her face, " 'O death, where is thy sting? O grave, where is thy victory? The sting of death is sin; and the strength of sin is the law. But thanks be to God, which giveth us the victory through our Lord Jesus Christ.' Oh, Father, I'd like to have that as the text for my funeral. I've told Vernon that. But I feel as if I'd like to shout it out. That's what the gospel is all about! We're all of us humans awfully afraid of death—because of our sinful natures—but knowing Christ—having Him wash us clean from our sin by faith in His blood—takes the sting and fear away. That's where the victory through Jesus Christ comes in. It's so wonderful!" The last was only a passionate whisper and then she sank into a silence which she did not break for the rest of the morning. He sat there, her hand in his for a long time.

After awhile he saw that she had dozed off and he gently released her hand.

A few days later she asked to be anointed for healing. She was back in the hospital again and Dan rode there with Vernon and the pastor and his assistant. Snow had fallen the day before and in the morning the sun came out with almost blinding brightness. Snowplows were still clearing some of the side roads, although the highway had been clear since the night before. They talked of casual things, none of them caring to touch too much on the purpose of their mission. Vernon and Dan were too close to it and both pastors respected their grief.

Dan had been present at another anointing service; Savilla had requested one before her death. There were those who questioned its validity, claiming it was too much like the Last Rites but if Helen found any significance in it he would be the last to deny her the ceremony. Although she had requested an anointing service, he knew she was fully prepared to die.

117

In any case it was a moving ceremony, broken only at the last with Vernon's sobbing. Helen's face was the most peaceful he had ever seen. She opened her eyes and, reaching out for Vernon's hand, gave him the same kind of smile she had given Dan that memorable moment a few days earlier. Vernon's sobs ceased.

Three days later she was dead.

10

$\mathbf{A}$ meadowlark called out from a tree at the far end of the lawn, a robin hopped across it nearer to Dan, and from across the north end of town came the sound of someone's power mower. He closed his eyes and let the sounds lull him, glad that his hearing was still good enough to let him hear a meadowlark at the same time he heard a power mower. He was sitting on the bench overlooking the grounds of the Home and, beyond that, the town that sloped to the south and east of the Home. Tulips bloomed along the borders where last fall the mums had been such a mass of color, and the lilacs were so plentiful in town that last evening when he had been out here he had smelled them on the breeze.

Oats had been planted long enough to be a healthy green in the fields and someone had come into the Home today and reported that they had seen a field of corn coming up. The farmer who owned the field south and west of the Home had been working in the field all day yesterday, presumably planting corn; modern machinery bore so little resemblance to what Dan had used on the farm that sometimes he was almost hard-pressed to determine what they were doing. Only when he drove past a field of the Old Order and saw them out with antiquated horse equipment could he tell at a glance what was being done.

He wondered if Vernon was already planting. This was Tuesday and he had not seen anything of him or Judy since Sunday, when he had been there for dinner after church services. He had joined them often since Helen passed away, although in February he had been laid up with pneumonia for the first time in his life. That had kept him confined to the Home for over a month. Evidently his time had not yet come, although death had taken away some of the residents. One morning in March, Veenie Kinsinger was found dead in her bed, having passed away in her sleep, and just two weeks ago Lydie Brenneman had died of a stroke. But his other close friends, James and Newt and John and Mandy, were still going strong. They were all around here somewhere; James had been sitting beside him until ten minutes ago when he left to go to town for a haircut. No doubt Newt was watching TV and John might be putting a puzzle together. Why anyone would want to sit inside and do those winter activities when they could be outside and smell the good earth and new-mown grass and lilacs and hear the meadowlarks sing was beyond him. But to each his own, he thought.

Catty-corner across the lots he saw Lizzie Miller in her garden, bending over and planting something. He wondered if Judy had planted some more things. It was hard for her to decide when was the right time to do some of those things. To be sure she had helped Helen some through the years but what with grade and high school and then four years of college, followed by a year in VS and then last year her job, really, when had she last been home to

120

help Helen through garden planting? Hardly ever, since Helen had always been well and active.

So this year she kept asking Vernon or Dan for advice. Vernon had been like most farm husbands—he knew his wife had a garden and he loved fresh garden stuff but he couldn't have told what kind of lettuce to plant or which peas produced the best if his life depended on it. And much of it was hazy in Dan's memory. He had helped Savilla after they moved to town, so he knew in a general way when to plant the stuff but he wasn't very sure of himself. Luckily, Judy was on good terms with the neighbor women and could turn to them for help.

Twice since Helen's funeral Lonnie had come up to see her. The first time she had brought him over to the Home to see Dan while he was convalescing from pneumonia, but the second time had been on Easter Sunday and Dan had been invited out for dinner. Each time he had been impressed with the young man's quiet good looks and grave personality. And each time it looked as if Judy were more in love. But as far as Dan knew, nothing had been settled between them.

Helen's death had saddened her daughter but at no time had Dan had the impression that the sorrow had been overwhelming. Was it her newfound love for Lonnie that still kept the twinkle in her eye and the spring in her walk? He rather thought so.

But if Judy was not overwhelmed with sorrow, Vernon was. Dan sighed as he thought of his son-in-law. All the weight he had lost had not been put back on, even if Judy was fast developing as a first-rate cook; His clothes hung on his frame and he was quieter than ever. Often half a day passed when they were together with no more than a dozen words spoken by each. Years ago such periods of silence would have made Dan nervous and he would have tried to fill them with talk, no matter how trivial, but life had taught him to respect the silence. So if Judy was not

121

with them to talk they sat together in silence and came to know each other better that way.

The robin he had seen a few minutes ago was tapping the ground for a worm, cocking his head to one side, and then tapping again. He watched him idly. It made him think of the robins that had followed in the old days when he was farming with a team and walking plow. Sometimes a regular flock of them hopped along behind him in the furrow ready to pick up any exposed worm. This robin now suddenly put his beak to the ground and jerked out a worm and flew away with it.

"Enjoying the sunshine, Dan?" Mandy's voice asked behind him and he turned slowly.

"I didn't know you were out here."

"I saw you through the window so I thought I'd come out and join you for a few minutes." She carried a sweater over her arm and carefully spread it on the bench before she sat down. They sat for a moment in silence.

"This is a beautiful place," Mandy said dreamily.

"I know."

"Only heaven could be more beautiful, it seems to me."

"You're prejudiced, Mandy. Have you ever lived anywhere else but here in Iowa?"

"No, but I've visited all over the country. In the years when Amos was the bishop of our church we went to conference every year and that took us from the East Coast to the West, from Canada to Florida. I think I've been in every state in the Union and in three of the provinces of Canada and Amos went to Europe, although I didn't go along."

Well! No one could say that Mennonites are stay-at-homes, he thought wryly.

"If you've got that record you beat me," he chuckled. "I've only hit half the states and never did get to Canada. But I can go Amos just as good. I went to Europe, too."

"Did you? Oh, yes, I remember. You went with Alta and

Jake to Mennonite World Conference, didn't you?"

"Uh-hum."

She sighed. "We traveled all over and yet liked Iowa best. But our grandchildren have started scattering. I have someone in ten different states now." She began to count. "Let's see, Indiana, Illinois, Michigan, Ohio, Pennsylvania, Virginia, Maryland, and one in Oregon, besides here in Iowa."

"They scatter, don't they?" he agreed.

"Yes, they do. Your children kind of did that, didn't they?"

"Yes, they did. But that's life. Can't always keep them under our roof."

"Many a time I look back and think those were our happiest times—when the children were small and I knew where they all were when bedtime came. Even if Amos was so busy with church work and gone a lot. We were young and together and we had faith in God—We couldn't have been happier."

"Oh, Mandy, you've forgotten a lot," he chided gently. "Don't you remember all of the church troubles and how some of the people of Upper Deer Creek wouldn't nod to anyone of Lower Deer Creek if they met on the road?"

"Oh, now that you mention it, yes. But that hurt has gone so long ago I don't even remember what it felt like. Maybe we were too self-righteous then, Dan. Maybe if we'd not been so proud of our humility we both would have joined the same conference."

"I've thought of that, too," he admitted. "And I suppose we at Lower Deer Creek were too impatient."

"It's too bad we didn't have the patience and compassion then that the Lord has taught us through the years. If we'd had the smarts when we were young just think what we could have made out of life!"

"It doesn't work out that way," he said. "Remember that old Pennsylvania Dutch saying, 'We get too young auldt and too auldt schmart? By the time we have the schmart we're ready for the grave.'"

"Well, the Lord knows His business. Maybe we'll need the 'schmarts' in heaven."

"I expect we will."

They lapsed into a companionable silence, then Mandy spoke again. "I got a letter from one grandson, the one that lives in Oregon, and he wants to come back for a visit in a few weeks. IMS is having a whole weekend of alumni celebration—my youngest daughter, Ella, mentioned it, too. She went there the first year it opened."

"So? Judy probably forgot to mention it."

"She's a dear girl, Dan."

"I think so."

"Is she still at home with Vernon?"

"Yes, she probably will be for a while. Unless she marries." He thought of Judy's growing love for Lonnie.

"Does she have a boyfriend?"

"Mandy, you may not believe this but she's going with old Christ C. Miller's grandson."

"Your cousin Christ. Is that right? And where's he from? Around here?"

"No, his folks moved to southern Iowa about fifteen-twenty years ago. But he came up to IMS for his senior year and Judy met him there."

"You mean she's been going with him all this while?"

"No, no. They only started that since last fall. Oh, I guess they've seen each other off and on but nothing was serious."

"So? Well, I wish her God's best, I'm sure."

o   o   o

By the end of the week the weather got colder and a drizzling rain set in—a million-dollar rain, farmers called it, since they'd had no moisture for two weeks and this should get the crops off to a fine start. Sunday morning it was still raining, a cold driving drizzle that made a mockery of

124

spring. One visitor at the Home claimed to have even seen a few flakes of snow.

Since his siege of pneumonia Dan was more cautious about the weather and elected to stay at the Home for worship services. Before he had gone to his home church whenever possible; there was always a load or two going out and it was easy to hitch a ride. However, some ministers always came to the Home for morning worship services. Many of those who regularly went to their own home churches sometimes elected to stay. Newt usually stayed, as did James Griffith, since there was no Baptist church in town, and John Schlabach had become so hard of hearing that he preferred staying of late, seating himself squarely in front of the preacher where he was sure to hear every word.

This morning the preacher was from one of the outlying congregations, a young man, not too long graduated from seminary. Dan had heard him before and had not been too impressed with the sermon but hoped he might get better with experience. This morning his first impression was not altered. Did he imagine it, or did these young preachers run all around Robin Hood's barn without saying anything definite, something you could sink your teeth into? Did they perhaps feel that old people were so far gone that they wanted only milk-toast for spiritual food? Maybe he was too old-fashioned and critical but the sermon they were hearing this morning was a far cry from the old "thus saith the Lord" type of messages some of the old-timers had preached. Even the pastor and assistant pastor of his own congregation could preach what Dan called a meat and potatoes spiritual meal.

He felt guilty with his thoughts and decided not to say anything about them to anyone but after dinner John came to sit beside him in the lounge, lowering himself stiffly to the same sofa.

"What'd you think of the sermon this morning, huh?" John asked.

Now he was in for it. "Well—it wasn't the best I've heard."

"What?"

"It wasn't the best sermon I've ever heard." He hoped in the general din their conversation would not be too noticeable.

"Humph," John snorted. "It was one of the worst I've ever heard."

"He's still young," Dan said. "Maybe he'll learn." He raised his voice loudly enough so that for once John heard him the first time.

"Well, I sure hope he does. What's wrong with our colleges? If they can't turn out better preachers we'd be better off if we went back to the old way and ordained by lot!"

"Do you think so?"

"I sure do! What would some of our old preachers like Jacob Swartzentruber and Joseph Gingerich and William K. Miller say about this modern stuff they preach nowadays? When have you last heard a hell-fire-for-sinners, washed-in-the-blood-of-Christ sermon?"

"Well-l-l. Not lately."

"You're right. Looks like to me that we broke away from any discipline that affects our outward appearance but we don't have anything solid to take its place. It's enough to make you sick, when you see these women running around in britches with their chopped-off hair and breaking their necks to keep up with the Joneses. And now they're coming in with jewelry and throwing away the covering— I tell you, if my mother and yours could see my grandchildren and yours they'd be sorry they ever begat their parents."

Dan thought of Ma, with her dark shawl and bonnet and the snowy white prayer cap tied under her chin with the wide self-tie, and then of Judy. John was right, in a sense.

"But you can't argue that we should go back to the old ways, though. Look at the Old Order—they try to but they're so wrapped up in legalism that they can't hear the gospel—"

"Yah, but they're still standing for a principle. They may not go at keeping it in the right way, but they still have the principle."

"What principle do you mean?"

"The principle of self-denial!" John said triumphantly. "We kicked that out somewhere along the line. We said it didn't mean dress and maybe it doesn't, but we don't know what it does mean so we ignore it completely. And if the preachers quit preaching the new birth and repentance from sin and the blood of Jesus Christ cleansing us from sin what have we got? A bunch of mealymouthed hypocrites that'll blow whichever way popular opinion blows."

"That's pretty strong medicine," Dan said.

"So what? I'm an old man that's got one foot in the grave and if I can't speak my piece now I never will. And if we don't get some better sermons I'm going to kick loose and tell some of these preachers and church leaders how I feel. I ain't got much to lose—I'm about dead anyway."

"You know, I think you're right," Dan said.

"What?"

"I think you're right."

"Right? Of course, I'm right."

Just then Dan caught sight of Judy coming through the entry with Lonnie. He half rose. "Here comes Judy."

"Huh?"

"Judy. My granddaughter." He indicated with his arm.

Old John turned toward the door. "Nice-looking couple. Engaged?"

"Not that I know of." He got up and went to meet them.

Judy looked puzzled, he thought as they greeted each other, not at all as if she were in an ecstasy of happiness to see Lonnie. It turned out that he had been in the community since Friday evening to attend the alumni celebration at IMS.

127

"You weren't in church this morning, were you, Grandpa?" she asked. "At least, I couldn't see you. I was going to take you home for dinner."

"No, child, when it kept on raining I decided I'd better stay here. I don't want pneumonia again if I can help it. Why don't we sit down or go to my room?"

"This is all right," Judy said. "I don't know how long we'll stay."

"Has it quit raining?" Dan asked.

"Yes. I think it's going to clear off and get cold. Maybe even freeze," Lonnie said.

"My, my, I hope not. That would be bad for the farmers and gardeners," Dan said. "Judy, did you get your tomato plants set out?"

"Yes, I did it Thursday. Do you suppose they'll freeze?"

"Did you cover them with hotcaps?"

"Uh-huh."

"They should be all right, unless it gets real cold. But I doubt if it will go below freezing. How are things in southern Iowa, Lonnie?"

"About like here." They went into a routine conversation about crops and climate and all the while the feeling grew stronger that not everything was going well with these two. He glanced keenly at Judy but she refused to meet his eyes. Neither did she hang onto every word Lonnie said, as she had the last time he had seen the two together.

After about half an hour of trivial conversation she rose. "Maybe we'd better go. We're tiring you, Grandpa. Have you had your afternoon nap yet?"

"I don't always take one," he said. "You don't have to hurry."

"Lonnie wants to leave before church time," she said.

"That will be a couple of hours," Lonnie said. "If you want to stay longer, Judy, I don't have to go for another hour." He said it very politely.

Plainly their relationship was under a strain. They sat for

128

another fifteen minutes and then Judy got up and slung her bag over her shoulder.

"Why don't we go over and see Carol and Jim Kinsinger?" she asked Lonnie. "Carol said last night to drop over and see them before you left."

"Did she? Okay." Lonnie got up, then put out his hand to Dan. "It's been nice seeing you again."

"Same here. Anytime you're close here just drop in and see me."

"Thank you. I just might do that."

He watched as they walked across the lounge to the entry. At the door Judy turned and smiled thinly. Even as he waved in return he thought that something had happened to them. They don't look like boy and girl friend to me.

11

That night the thermometer dropped down to thirty. Very little corn had come up as yet but tender tomato and pepper plants received a blow, especially as the sun warmed up by noon and wilted any plant prone to freeze. The strawberry crop would be cut in half this year, people said, and as for apples and pears, there would be none of those.

But the community snapped back like a rubber band; there had been late frosts before and no one had starved. Most people were subconsciously aware of this, even those lamenting frozen plants. The greenhouses in the area did a double business as people flocked to them for replacements.

Judy's plants escaped the worst of the freeze, since the garden was sheltered by the buildings and the tenderest plants covered with hotcaps, Vernon explained, when he dropped in to see Dan toward the middle of the week. And when Dan asked about Lonnie, Vernon was vague. Maybe Judy and Lonnie had had a quarrel, but he hadn't noticed,

130

he said. Judy hadn't said anything. Dan gave up prodding. If Judy had a burden she could always come to him.

He saw nothing of her that week. The rain had given new impetus to grass and shrubs and flowers and they grew as if in a jungle. The late tulips came out, and bridal wreath bushes broke into splotches of white all over town; the white bridal wreath fronted by blazing tulips sent more than one fan for a camera. The rain must have washed the fragrance from the lilacs, though, for one could no longer breathe it in on the evening air.

Fannie May was voluble about her mother's yard and garden. Luckily she hadn't transplanted the houseplants yet, she told Dan, or they would surely all be frozen. But the tulips were so pretty! And the bridal wreath! And Anna Sue was so good at helping her mother, it made Fannie May feel less guilty about not staying at home and helping because her mother's heart was causing more trouble this spring.

Dan let her ramble on, his mind only hearing enough to give him a sense of what she was saying. Besides, if he began a real conversation she would never get his room cleaned and he wanted to finish a letter to Alta. He finally picked up his writing tablet and the stamped, addressed envelope and escaped to the lounge. This time of the day visitors were at a minimun and if Newt or John or James or Mandy didn't run into him he might be able to get the letter in the morning mail.

He had finished it and stuck it into the slot at the front desk and was turning away when he saw Judy coming in the front door. She caught sight of him and came over, smiling in a way that made him want to take her in his arms.

"Why, Judy, how does it happen you're here?"

"I had to run in for some groceries. And I thought I'd plant a few more tomatoes, so I was going to stop at the greenhouse and get some." As usual on weekdays she was dressed in blue jeans and involuntarily he thought of John.

131

"Can I take you out for supper tonight?" she asked.

"Why I don't know why not. Is your father going?"

"No, that's why it suits tonight. He's been invited out and I don't especially care to go with him. You and I haven't gone out for supper since way last fall."

Not since the beginning of Helen's illness, he thought, but neither of them said so.

"Why, yes, I can, Judy. What time?"

"Oh, around six. I guess. Daddy's supposed to be at his place by seven but I hate to make you wait so long for your supper. Don't you eat at five-thirty?"

"Yes, but don't let that bother you. I'll be ready anytime you come. Where do you want to go?"

"I suppose down here at the Town House. Is that okay with you?"

"Fine. Anyplace you want to go."

"I'll see you then." She turned and left again.

As he headed down the hall he wondered what to do. He had no new reading matter—surely the mail would bring some again—and it was too cool to go outdoors. He saw nothing of John or Newt or James. Mandy was probably piecing quilt blocks in her room and, as far as he was concerned, there as nothing on TV worth looking at this time of the day. He supposed he could go up to his room and write to Duane or Guy but the former had called last Sunday evening and he had written to Guy at the beginning of the week and as yet had received no answer. Most of the activities planned for them were in the afternoon—slide presentations, games, crafts, or Bible study—but the mornings were left open for the residents to do as they wished. Many of the women, who were able, had running projects going continually; one hour it was knitting, the next crocheting, or tatting, or embroidery; and the next time you looked in they were piecing quilts for children, for grandchildren, nieces, nephews, and so on. There was so much more to keep an older woman occupied than an older man.

He had no hobbies himself beyond reading and talking, and never had. Newt went in for puzzles and John for checkers; both of these bored him. James loved to play the piano but he was nowhere in sight now. Dan sighed and went back to his room again. He saw thankfully that Fannie May had finished and gone.

o   o   o

He was sitting in the lounge waiting for Judy. From the dining room came the clink of silverware and the hum of conversation as the supper hour drew to a close. The lounge was deserted and he sat alone watching a nature film on TV. He wished there were more nature programs, then one might be able to see good in having a TV in the lounge. He glanced at his watch. Almost five-thirty. Judy wouldn't be here for another thirty minutes.

The nature film drew to a close and then came the news. He never cared for the news on TV; he preferred getting it from the newspaper and since he was usually at the supper table at this time, he seldom saw it.

Judy came in just as the national news came to an end. He was glad to see her, both for herself and because the news made him uneasy and sad. With all the efforts of men in his lifetime, it didn't look as if they had made the world a better place to hand over to Judy's generation.

"Were you waiting long?" she asked, as he pulled on his light sweater that had been draped over the arm of his chair.

"No. Not waiting, especially. I thought I'd watch the news until you came. Usually we're eating supper and I almost never see it in the evening. And after seeing it now, I don't believe I'm missing very much."

She helped him settle his sweater in place around his shoulders. "You get the same thing at ten."

"But we're in bed by then." He unhooked his cane from the arm of his chair and said, "I'm ready."

She preceded him to the door and pushed it open, wait-

133

ing for him to go through. She was dressed in a pink flowered dress with a short sleeve plain color sweater to match. Her long hair hung over her shoulders, held out of her face by a plain barette. Her face looked tired, he thought, as he met her eyes after they had both gone through the door. Her smile looked sadder than it had when Helen died.

She linked her arm through his. "This is a pretty evening again, Grandpa."

"Yes it is, child. Any of your daddy's corn up yet?"

"Yes, I saw rows of new corn in the field across the road this morning. And this afternoon I saw a blossom on my peas."

Her face lighted momentarily.

"Really?" Dan said. "I didn't think the freeze would do those too much damage. Peas can take it. And your tomato plants are still growing?"

"Uh-hum. I haven't taken the hotcaps off though. I don't dare."

"No, I'd keep them on for another week. Maybe by then they'll be so big you'll have to take them off."

They were in the car by now and Judy backed away from the curb and turned toward the street. Children were playing all through town, he noted, playing baseball or biking or just rolling around on the ground like little puppies. At one corner two little girls with their doll buggies were talking. They looked for all the world like their mothers, he thought, as one bent down into the buggy, obviously checking her make-believe baby. Judy drove slowly, both because of the darting children and because she enjoyed watching them as much as he did. They shared a laugh when they saw one small boy trying to run with a puppy tugging at his pant leg.

They were soon at the restaurant since it was only half a dozen or so blocks away. The restaurant had a special dining room that was open to the public only in the evening (one done up with the Amish theme—not appreciated by the Amish), and he and Judy came down here several times a year. The food was well cooked in the Amish way, which was no surprise because Amish ladies cooked it. It was generally held in good-natured derision by the local rural residents. After all, most of them had Amish background and ate food like that every day; if they wanted something special they went to the city or Cedar Rapids or the Amana Colonies. But tourists loved it and most of the trade who patronized it came from out of town.

There was no one in the restaurant they knew and they chose a small table in the corner—half a room away from a large tableful of strangers, evidently a family party. As they waited for a waitress to come for their order Dan looked at the large mural on the wall. It depicted scenes from Amish life—an Amish woman and her little daughter, an Amish rig going down the road, the horse smartly trotting and the carriage one of the top buggies that had become popular since the Second World War. It amused him faintly; they needn't tell him the Amish didn't change—that buggy would never have been seen on the road at the time of the telephone split. Tops were not even allowed on them before the nineteen hundreds. But surprisingly the rig was true in most details.

After they had given the waitress their orders he directed his attention to Judy. "You look tired, Judy. Are you working too hard?"

"Oh, I don't know. I've been very busy, but I don't care. I like to keep busy."

"Your mother used to complain all last fall of taking care of that big house."

"It is big. Daddy and I rattle around in it alone. The boys are coming home after graduation so we'll need more room."

"Are they coming to stay?"

"Not for long. Jim has the chance of a position for summer school and Gary plans to go with some volunteer work group for about six weeks."

The waitress came with their salad; she knew both of them well and no wonder, since she was one of Mandy's grandchildren, and she was anxious to please.

They talked little among themselves until she had brought them the rest of the order. Then he asked, "Did Lonnie get home all right?"

Instantly there was a guarded look on her face. "I suppose so. I didn't hear that he was killed anyway."

He looked at her keenly, his fork in the air. "Has something happened between you two?"

"Nothing ever did 'happen' as you suggest. But we can't see eye to eye—on some things—" she finished lamely, not meeting his eyes.

"I'm sorry to hear that."

"Why?" she asked.

"Well—he was such a nice young man. And I guess because of his grandfather—"

"You hoped there would be a linking of our two families?" her voice hardened.

"No. Not especially. There were some things old Christ told me the last time I talked with him. He was so superior and so dead sure his way was right—I guess I was glad to see that Lonnie had broken out of that—"

"Who says he has?" Her voice was still hard. "As far as I'm concerned Lonnie is like his old grandfather."

"So? In what way?"

"Dead sure he's right."

"In what way?"

She paused and then continued, "Grandpa, have you ever had a moment's doubt about our denomination?"

He thought of last Sunday morning and his conversation with John afterward. "Why do you ask?"

"Because Lonnie sure voiced a lot of them. Of course he's been brainwashed by the Baptists—"

136

"Careful what you say, girl," he cautioned. "The Baptists claim the same spiritual heritage that we do."

"They do? Really?"

"Yes, they do. I didn't realize it until I read the book *The Indomitable Baptists.* I often wondered why there were no Anabaptists in Great Britain since they spread all over the continent but that book explained why."

"Why weren't there?"

"Well, in the general persecution some of them fled across the Channel and over there people just dropped the 'Ana' and called them Baptists."

"I didn't know that," she said slowly.

"Few people do. But they claim Conrad Grebel and Georg Blaurock and the other Anabaptists as their spiritual fathers same as we do."

"Maybe we don't have that general knowledge but I don't think the Baptists do either. In fact, that was one of the worst criticisms Lonnie had. He said our denomination keeps harping about our Anabaptist forefathers as if they could give us 'new life in Christ,' as he put it."

"So?"

She laid her fork down and buried her face in her hands for a moment. "Oh, Grandpa, when Mother died I grieved but I guess I thought I still had Lonnie—"

"I thought it seemed like it—"

"But now he's—I mean, I broke with him—and he cast such doubts on our denomination. I don't have Mother and I don't have him and now I don't have any faith—" Her voice was thick.

"Tell me what he said, honey," Dan said gently, thankful the waitress was busy with the large family party.

But instead of telling him she gave her eyes a hard rub and picked up her fork again. "I went to church and Sunday school all my life, I gave a year of my life in Voluntary Service, and I don't have anything that can get me through this—"

"The Lord can," he said, so softly that she might not have heard it if she had so much as clinked her fork.

"Yes—the Lord can—but that is just it," she said in an intense whisper. "Where is He? Or who is He? Is He the Lord Lonnie knows—that the Baptists know? Or is He the Lord the—the Anabaptists know?"

"Child, child, I would hope and pray it would be one and the same. Is Christ divided?" Unconsciously he quoted Paul the apostle in 1 Corinthians.

"To hear Lonnie talk we Anabaptists aren't even serving Him." She said in bitterness of spirit. "He says our denomination worships our forefathers instead of Christ and makes more of our heritage than we do of the new birth. He said we seem to feel that we are born God's people automatically and that we hold Menno Simons a greater authority than the Apostle Paul. He said if persons come along and profess to be conscientious objectors we give the right hand of fellowship whether they believe Christ died for their sins or not. And he said we act as if talking about sins and the need for repentance were dirty words that you shouldn't mention in polite company—"

"Those are strong words." By now he too had laid down his fork.

"Grandpa, do you believe them?" It was the cry of someone who felt her whole foundation crumble.

Did he? He thought again of last Sunday. "When have you last heard a hell-fire-for-sinners, washed-in-the-blood-of-Christ sermon?" John had asked.

"Do you? Is something wrong with our denomination." She almost pleaded with him to say no.

"Judy, when it comes to the basic fundamentals of our Mennonite Church I can honestly say I want nothing better. Read our confession of faith and compare it with the Bible and it stands firm. By the way, I've read confessions of faith of other denominations and yes, even the Baptists, and basically they read about the same. But I'll be the last one to say that nothing is wrong with my beloved denomination."

"Well, what is it? Is Lonnie right?"

"He's on the edge looking in and I'm on the inside. Our perspectives may not be quite the same—"

"Oh, Grandpa, now you're running all around Robin Hood's barn. Give it to me straight. Is there something wrong?"

"Yes."

"What is it?"

He thought a minute. "I'm afraid God's got too many grandchildren in it."

"Oh, Grandpa, what do you mean?"

"Honey, it's the same problem all denominations have, especially those with strong cultural and ethnic backgrounds such as ours. The children join the church on their parents' faith—they've never really met Jesus Christ personally. They mouth the words and believe them in their heads but they have never committed themselves to Jesus Christ in their inmost being—in their souls."

She picked up her fork and dug around in her mashed potatoes and gravy.

"When did you do that?" she asked.

"When I was twenty years old. Then I experienced the new birth. Life was never the same afterward."

"Maybe that's what's wrong with me," she said after a moment.

"Judy, if you've never asked Jesus Christ to come into your heart, nothing is keeping you from doing it right now."

She laid down her fork again. "I don't even know how to go about it."

"How would you ask me to come into your house?"

She met his eyes. "Just ask you to come in."

"Then ask Him."

She propped her elbows on the table and buried her face

139

in her hands. "Jesus Christ, come into my heart. Grandpa says You'll come in if I ask and I'm asking You now. I've got to have something to cling to."

It might not be orthodox, he thought, but he had no doubt of her heartfelt sincerity. His eyes were wet and he got out his handkerchief and blew his nose.

"God bless you, honey," he said softly. She reached across the table and grabbed his hand. "Thanks, Grandpa."

12

He was too thrilled to sleep; the happening this evening had touched him too deeply. When Judy dropped him off after they left the restaurant, he had gone right to his room, not wanting any of the preciousness of it to be lost in conversation with anyone. But neither could he settle down and read nor listen to the radio, even if he turned it to a Christian FM station. Finally, he sat down in his rocking chair and leaned back, his hands clasped together at the back of his head, and gave himself up to the events of the evening.

It seemed a miracle that he could have been present when this most beloved grandchild totally committed herself to Jesus Christ. He prayed now that she might find a new and deeper meaning to life and the fellowship of other believers—the new birth Jesus had called it in speaking to Nicodemus.

As so often happened his thoughts went back to the time

when he had made his own commitment. He had been courting Savilla steadily for almost a year although it was a wonder she put up with him. His inward misery was so great, what with his steadily growing conviction, that he was utterly unfit to keep company with decent people such as she was. How she ever kept from suspecting some of his deeds he never knew but even as he loathed himself he was sick with fear that she would find out and reject him.

But one fall the Werey Church was holding a week of meetings with a young evangelist who later went out as a missionary. Savilla suggested going, a surprising thing, since the majority of the Laplanders considered the Werey group too progressive and her father was no exception. He felt almost numb as he drove down to pick up Savilla at her home. He had despaired of his sin so long that he had reached the point of apathy.

There was strict segregation of the sexes in those days. He dropped Savilla off at the women's side of the building. Then he toyed with the wild idea of going somewhere to end it all, but the strong teaching he had received against suicide kept him from it. He drove to the end of the hitching racks, way down at the bottom of the hill, and tied his horse there before he made his miserable way to the meeting.

The meetinghouse was already almost full of people he knew, since the Deer Creek and Laplander young people freely mingled. He shook hands with the young men or nodded if they happened to be already seated and caught his eye. Almost automatically his eyes located Savilla over on the women's side where she was sitting with some of her girl friends toward the front.

He had never attended an evangelistic service before and hardly knew what to expect. But as the young minister began preaching it was almost as if he were pointing his finger directly at Dan Brenneman. As far as Dan could have told, there was no one else in the building except the young

142

preacher and himself. For his text the preacher had chosen the third chapter of the Gospel of John. Even though this text was preached on regularly every spring the first Sunday after communion, to remind those who had reached the age of accountability of the necessity of it, Dan had never had the idea of a new birth presented so clearly as that evening. "This is it," some voice seemed to be telling him. When the invitation was given he was one of the first to respond.

Even though he went forward not much was said, except the evangelist told him he would come see him the next day. But at least he had enough peace of mind to sleep well for the first time in months. The next day the young preacher came to see him, accompanied by one of the ministers of the Werey Church. Then he confessed the lies he had told, the articles he had stolen, and his love of filthy stories. When the evangelist had finished dealing with him, he had a peace in his heart such as he had never enjoyed before. His life was so changed from then on that there was never any doubt in his mind that the new birth had taken place in his heart.

But there was restitution to be made; the Holy Spirit would not let him rest until everything was made right that it was humanly possible to correct. How he had dreaded to confess to the Benders the things he had pilfered. But God bless good, kind John Bender. When Dan came to him with the stolen things over his arm the old man took him in his arms and the two mingled their tears. From that time on it was as if John took the place of the father Dan had lost.

And now the irony of it came back. For months he had been going with Savilla in his unconverted state. But now that he had been converted, and through the Werey Church at that, Savilla's father almost made them break up. Even though the young people still mingled, their elders were fast drawing apart to where there could be no more fellowship. Bishop Werey was looked upon with deep suspicion and distrust by the hard-core Old Order, of which Savilla's father was one of the worst, and he was not about to have one of his daughters date a young man who had made a public stand in that church. And after Dan had gone the rounds to make restitution and word of some of his former deeds leaked out it was even worse. It was only after dear old John Bender had had a chance talk with him that her father grudgingly consented to let them keep on going steady. Dan hoped that he had never regretted it; at least their relationship as father-in-law and son-in-law had been fairly satisfactory.

Looking back now, Dan could see that that commitment had been the thin edge of the wedge as far as his relationship to his cousin Christ was concerned. And yet, far be it from him to infer that Christ had never made a commitment to the Lord Jesus Christ, since he had settled down to be a model young man, had married one of Daniel Gingerich's granddaughters, and supported the organized church faithfully all his life. It was just that Christ had grown steadily more conservative while he, Dan, had never felt that material progress was a thing to be shunned, but rather that it could be used to the honor and glory of God as long as there was no moral principle involved.

But now Christ's grandson had been the one to deliver his scathing denunciation of the denomination to Judy. Once more her words came back to him with all her bitterness and fear, "He says our denomination worships our heritage instead of Jesus Christ—"

Did he? He looked back at Ma, at Pa, at the old bishops and ministers who had served so ably within his lifetime— William K. Miller, Gideon Yoder, Noah D. Yoder, Peter Swartzentruber, Jacob Swartzentruber, and many more, including Grandpa Brenneman and all those who had first helped organize the church. Did he venerate them more than he did Christ his Lord? He did not think so; they were poor weak humans just as he was. Several had quick tempers, one or two had had domineering personalities, and

144

as far as Menno Simons, Conrad Grebel, or Georg Blaurock were concerned, he admired and respected them for having the courage to stand for their convictions, but far be it for him to hold them any higher than any other mortal. And yet, he could not deny that Lonnie might have some legitimate complaint. Once again he thought of what he had told Judy, and he heaved a heavy sigh as he did so. There were too many people in the church who were God's grandchildren. It would be easy for them to set their sights no higher than the human founders of the church. At that admission a heavy burden settled on his heart.

Ah, his dear church! His dear, dear people! "O God!" he prayed, "bring a great renewing to our people! Let them get their eyes on Thee rather than on poor weak humans. Judy said Lonnie feels our people act as if sin and the need of the new birth were dirty words that are not to be mentioned in polite society. Dear God, please open their understanding to this sin of pride. Thy Word says Thou resisteth the proud but giveth grace to the humble. Dear Lord, I love my people, but I'm afraid Lonnie isn't altogether wrong. Renew my people for Thy great mercy's sake. Amen."

＊　＊　＊

The roses were beginning to bloom again; it seemed to him that everytime he came out to look at them a few more buds had opened. A gorgeous red one was his favorite; he wished he could have raised roses such as this when he was still gardening. But try as he might he had never been as successful as they were here at the Home; it must be the soil or the lay of the ground. Anyway, he was glad for these and thankful for the bench placed so that he could sit in the shade and feast his eyes on them.

For the shade felt good again. Old people who only last week sought the sun now took to the shade since the thermometer had soared into the nineties. Strawberry time often brought the first hot weather and this year was no exception. Gardens were producing well again this year and housewives were proudly comparing yields. When late summer came and they had to work long hours to can and freeze, some of the pride would give way to frustration, Dan knew, but that didn't dampen their enthusiasm now.

The corn and soybeans looked good, he thought, his eye roving over the cornfield south of the Home grounds. They used to say if corn was knee-high by the Fourth of July it was doing well, but it looked as though it would be shoulder-high by the Fourth this year. Last Sunday when he had gone home with Vernon and Judy he had seen that Vernon's crops looked as good as always. Now that Jim had earned his doctorate, he had come home and was helping for a few weeks before he went to his teaching position at the University of Missouri. Gary had accepted a short-term VS assignment at a school for retarded children in Colorado, still not ready to settle down to his lifework, whatever that would be.

Dan saw James Griffith come slowly down the walkway toward him. His eyes softened. James wasn't at all well these days; his heart was causing him pain with worsening angina pectoris. Only on warm still days such as this could he stand to be out. Any cold wind made his heart work harder.

"Come over here and sit by me, James," he called. "It's nice and warm and there's no wind."

"I was hoping you would say so." James had never had a loud voice and now it was softer than ever. His long, thin face was pale, but then he had not worked out in the sun since he left the old Nebraska homestead as a boy of eighteen, hiring out first as a delivery boy in a hardware store in Council Bluffs and later going into his own plumbing business. All this Dan had learned in the countless reminiscences exchanged since they had both become residents of the Home.

James, never without his cane, lowered himself to the bench beside Dan and carefully hung it over the back. Now that the weather had turned so warm Dan left his own cane hanging on the closet door.

"Sit down and soak up the sun and enjoy God's and the Home's roses," Dan said.

"They are lovely, aren't they?" James assented. "You know, no man needs be ashamed of loving flowers if the Lord loved them."

"That's true. But whoever has the idea that liking flowers is sissy should have known my father. He loved 'em and I can't think of anyone less of a sissy than he was."

"Really?"

"Oh, looking back I know how he loved us but he surely didn't believe in showing us affection. He didn't even bother to praise us if we did a job well. We just knew that we'd better do it right or we'd get 'it.' 'It' was usually a whipping." He chuckled a little. "You know, according to our modern child psychologists I should have ended up a delinquent."

"How so?" James asked, a faint smile on his face.

"Why my mother died when I was ten and Father married again a year or so later and then he was killed when I was a young buck just at the place where I thought I knew it all. And we never had any of the advantages people give their children nowadays; I barely had enough education to teach me to read and write and figure."

"Oh, well, most of the other people you associated with were in the same boat," James pointed out.

"Yes, well, that's true. I guess I never felt out of place because we were all like that. But my father did have a little more education than I did, enough so he could teach school for a couple of years."

"Mine couldn't do more than sign his name," James said. "That's why he wanted his children to have more. He pinched and skimped and sent all four of us boys through academy which would be about like high school now, I guess. Of course we boys had to help pay our way, which

147

was why I started working in a hardware store. But my three sisters never did get more than the country school could give them." He smiled wryly.

"Women's lib hadn't caught on yet," Dan said.

"Not in things like that. But they all married well and ended up being wealthier than any of us boys so I guess justice won out."

They were silent for a moment. The distant sounds of the town around them were like soothing background music: the soft hum of traffic on the highway to the west of them, the muted roar of downtown traffic, the distant shrieks of junior league rooters in the ball park. The maintenance man was mowing the lawn on the other side of the Home and the sound ebbed and flowed as he mowed behind a cottage and then came to the front again.

"You know, our forefathers were a hardy lot, according to our modern standards," Dan began again. "We don't realize how hard they had to work just to exist in those days."

"I know," James said.

"I remember when my brother Jacob was twelve years old he broke his arm but Pa didn't think it was serious enough to take him to the doctor. We didn't realize how bad it was until it began to grow crooked. Jake favored it for a long time, but he never fussed. I guess he knew it wouldn't do any good. Of course, the nearest doctor was over twenty miles away at Iowa City and in those days you didn't go to the doctor unless it was absolutely necessary."

"That's the way it was on the homestead," James agreed. "One year we had scarlet fever and one little brother died and Ma and Pa just doctored us themselves. I don't know how close our nearest doctor was—maybe fifty miles."

"But our parents' generation were God-fearing men and women. Their spoken word was more binding than many a written, witnessed, and notorized agreement is nowadays."

"That's true. Pa rented a half-section from a man who

lived in Omaha and in all the ten years of their dealings together I don't think they ever had more than their spoken agreement as their bond."

"If our parents were like that, and I'm sure you wanted to be, and I know I always wanted to deal fair and square and I tried to pass it on to my children, what has happened? Somewhere along the line someone failed."

"Dan, each generation must make a fresh commitment to the truth," James said. "We can live for the Lord in our own lives in our generation and we can tell the next one about the way, but only they can respond. I wish sometimes we could live for the Lord in our children's stead but it doesn't work out that way. Each generation has to be born into right standing with God through Christ."

"Oh, I know," Dan said sadly. He thought of what he had told Judy that memorable night over a month ago—that God had too many grandchildren in the church.

"God doesn't have any grandchildren, you know," James said, almost as if he had read his thoughts.

"How did you know what I was thinking?" Dan asked humorously. "I was telling Judy a while ago that that was what was wrong with our denomination—"

"What? That God has too many grandchildren in it?"

"Yes. People who have heard the gospel from their elders but have never made a personal commitment to it."

"That's not a failing just of your church." James smiled sadly. "I'm afraid the Baptists are just as bad."

"It troubles me," Dan said. "If only they could see it!"

"I know. I feel the same way."

13

Fannie May was cleaning the room; already she had been reminded to get to work but still she made only halfhearted swipes with the dust mop. Usually he left the room so she would not be distracted with talk but today he was writing letters and, since it was raining, he could not take his tablet and pen outside to do it. Strawberry time had come and gone, raspberries were ripening, the oats was turning and corn was already shoulder-high. In town the streets swarmed with children, and their shrieks enlivened the Home grounds, like the chatter of birds. The days had been hot and dry until early this morning when the rumble of thunder had presaged rain. It was still raining so all activity had to be confined to indoors.

He had received a letter from Alta the day before and while he was in the mood for writing letters he decided to write Duane and Guy, and then if he felt like it, he would write to Gary, too.

"I wish they'd let her alone," Fannie was saying. "Those preachers have done nothing but pick on Anna Sue ever since she joined church."

"What's wrong with her now?" Dan asked.

"Yes, what is? Just because she's been wearing rayon stockings in this hot summer weather they came down last night to pick on her again. It makes me so provoked! Sometimes I wouldn't blame her if she left the church!"

"You mean you're not supposed to wear rayon stockings? What's wrong with rayon?"

"Oh, my no, we can't wear them! I don't know what's wrong with rayon. Some old lady who had ugly legs probably decided that if she didn't wear thin stockings then nobody else could either. Oh, I tell you, some of those old women watch us young girls like hawks! They're always criticizing our dress."

"In what way?"

"Oh, our dresses are too short or the colors too flashy or the material too fancy or we wear our coverings too far back or some such thing. They especially watch the real young girls, like Anna Sue. Even Mom's getting disgusted with them."

"You mean they keep picking on the girls for things like that? What do they do with someone who really falls into sin, the kind the Scriptures talk about—lying or cheating or adultery or gossip?"

"Hah! I'll tell you what they do. If the right one does it he can get by with anything. Just for instance, the son of one of the bishops made a confession last spring before communion for sleeping with his girlfriend but nobody says anything about that. They don't pick on him as much as they do on Anna Sue about rayon stockings."

"Well, that shouldn't be." Dan shook his head. "Surely, though, if someone is guilty of something the Bible definitely says is sin your people will deal with it."

"Oh, sure, if Anna Sue did she'd be kicked out in a hurry,

but if the preacher's children or those of the important members did the same thing they'd let them get by without saying anything. It makes me so provoked!" she repeated.

He felt sorry for her. If it helped her to unburden, he didn't want to walk out but yet he knew one of the cardinal rules of the Old Order was never to carry stories of church troubles to an outsider. Fannie May would probably get a sharp rebuke if the preachers found out she was telling tales.

"I don't believe you're supposed to be telling me these things," he reminded her.

"Oh, I know, but I'm that provoked. I wish they'd let her alone!"

She finally got the room cleaned after the second reminder from her supervisor to get to work. Dan sat and pondered her outburst after she was gone. He had never seen her so upset before. He didn't know enough about women's hose to know what kind of stockings Fannie May herself wore but evidently she felt that Anna Sue should wear what she liked, as long as she was modest.

How mixed up things can get, he thought. He agreed with Fannie May, it was not right to emphasize restrictions of men above the restrictions of the Scripture.

And yet, had not that been one reason for the break those long years ago? He remembered an article he had read within the past year from his stack of old magazines. The article by Daniel Kauffman in a yellowed issue of *Herald of Truth* told about his visit to the Iowa settlement. They hold more to the restrictions of men than the restrictions of Scripture, Kauffman had said. He reported that the wearing of buttons, a restriction of men, was frowned upon more than the wearing of jewelry. There would be many nowadays who did not even feel that the latter should be restricted, he knew. Nevertheless, in those days before mass production only the well-to-do could afford expensive ornaments and jewelry and he could well see the principle

152

of self-denial in it. Then, too, Kauffman had said that the Iowa people forbade new customs and practices without regard to their relation to the gospel.

New customs and practices—he leaned back in his chair and once more pondered the controversy of the telephone split. The teenagers and young children of today who used phones so casually, knowing how to dial almost before they can count, these young ones could never comprehend the distrust and suspicion with which that invention was regarded when it first came out, especially among a group of people who shied away from the world around them.

By 1895 it had already found its way among the members of the Werey Church, along with top buggies, picture taking, and so forth—things frowned on by the conservative Old Order in Lapland but yet not exactly forbidden. The main complaint against it was that one had to be a member of a mutual company to have one. In joining a secular company one became yoked with unbelievers, church leaders pointed out. The matter became so much a matter of controversy that advice was finally sought from leaders of other areas. The matter was resolved by asking that the church members rent their telephones from the company.

But the telephone had not come in so easily among the Deer Creek districts and was even yet strictly forbidden among the Lapland Old Order. Why had it been so painful? It had divided families so that the breach had continued for years—even now the results of individual choices were not healed.

Witness himself and Christ. Even now after all these years he could feel the heartache when they too had come to a parting of their ways. After he had made his public commitment to Jesus Christ, his companionship with his cousin had continued but with a difference; Dan no longer cared to do those things of which he was now so ashamed. But Christ had settled down a little, too. He had fallen in love with the girl who was to become his wife and he was

153

anxious to impress both her and her parents.

Had Christ ever personally committed himself to the Lord? Dan wondered. He didn't know. Surely it was not for him to judge, he thought. To all appearances Christ had settled down and supported the church and after he was married he had been no worse or better than his peers. He attended every service, he led in the singing, he taught Sunday school classes if called upon, all things Dan did, too.

But Christ had gradually become more strict, insisting more on the letter of the *Audnung* than the spirit of the Scriptures. The two couples were together often in their young, married life; they had wed the same year, moved into the same neighborhood, and each welcomed babies that first year. To Dan and Savilla had come Alta and for Christ and Katie it had been the oldest of a large family. One could point out that Christ might have been more inclined to be conservative because his father-in-law was and there might be a point in that. Certainly Christ's two sisters and four brothers had all stayed with the Deer Creek congregations and all of Katie's family had moved to Lapland after the split. In the end, though, over half of their families had ended up either at the Werey Church or waited another generation and joined one of the newer progressive churches.

But his mind went back to the difficult years just prior to the telephone split. By the time he and Savilla were married a number of families had installed telephones in their homes, some joining the mutual company and some merely renting the phones. He had often wondered since if some of the hard feelings couldn't have been avoided if it hadn't been for the abrasive personalities of the major participants. Although a very capable man, even his staunchest supporters had to admit that Jacob F. Swartzentruber did not always consider other people's ideas. And the long-standing antagonism between his family and the Gingerich family, whose grandfather had been silenced as a minister by

154

Jacob's grandfather had not helped matters. But whatever the contributing factors, the split caused a major upheaval among the Deer Creek congregations.

He remembered that for a whole year efforts had been made to heal the growing breach. On more than one Sunday ministers from other congregations had been present trying to work out a compromise. Some hot words were exchanged between Bishop Swartzentruber and the members and for each word spoken openly probably dozens had been said in private, including those exchanged between himself and Christ. One afternoon in early spring he had gone to Joetown, officially known as Amish, for some groceries for Savilla, riding over on horseback as he often did. Even now he could see the trees on each side of the path that cut through the thick timber from the church corner to the little town. He could feel the warm, moist, southeast wind on his face and smell the fresh scent of thawing earth. After purchasing his groceries and stowing them in a gunnysack which he tied on the saddle, he had cut across to see Christ, a different route home than the way he had come but only a little farther. He hated the growing estrangement between himself and Christ. It seemed incredible that the two who had been closer than brothers ever since they were old enough to recognize each other should be separated by the telephone issue. But of late they had talked of little but the weather when they met at services. During the winter the couples had not exchanged visits once or twice a month as they had the previous two years of their marriages. It troubled Dan. Wasn't there some way they could talk out their differences? That's why he wanted to talk to Christ on this afternoon.

He gave a piercing whistle as he came on the little farm, a familiar way of letting Christ know he was coming. He caught a glimpse of his cousin at the shop door and he rode his horse across the yard and slung the reins over the fence post.

"Busy?" he called, Christ having disappeared into the shop again before he dismounted.

"Hello. Where'd you come from? Yeah, I thought I'd clean out the shop and get my machinery ready so I can get in the fields as soon as spring is here." Did he imagine it, or was Christ not exactly pleased to see him?

"I had to go to Joetown to get some things for Savilla so I thought I'd stop in and see how you were."

"So?"

"Yah. Seems like I hardly get a chance to talk to you anymore. We don't get together so often."

"Yah. Well, we find that taking two babies out at night isn't as easy as taking one, or none. Katie's afraid they'll get sick. They've had some bad colds this winter and she missed church a lot. So I guess if she wasn't with me I didn't stay around and talk." He was sorting nails and he kept his eyes on his task.

"Yeah. Well, Savilla and I have a lot to be thankful for. Alta hasn't been sick all winter."

"So? That's good."

There was an awkward pause. Dan had the feeling that Christ was holding him at arm's length.

"What do you think of allowing the telephones?" Dan asked abruptly.

Instantly Christ looked up and met his eyes and there was an unmistakable hostility in his gaze. "I don't think much of it."

Even though he had opened fire, so to speak, Dan wasn't expecting this reaction. "Why not? I would say it's no worse than some of the other things we have allowed. It could be mighty handy in an emergency."

Slowly and deliberately Christ went back to sorting nails. "That can be argued, yes. But God is always ready to take care of us without any fancy new inventions. If our fathers and grandfathers got along without them, what need have we for them?"

156

"Well, yes, sure they got along without them—because they had to, that's why. But don't tell me they wouldn't have been glad to use them if they could have. It would be a big help in getting hold of a doctor. Why when Alta was coming I spent three hours tracking the doctor down; it's a wonder she wasn't born before he got there. That could have been awful, as sick as Savilla was. She almost died."

"If she had, it would have been God's will. Any newfangled invention like a telephone wouldn't have kept her from dying."

"Well, yes, but I could have been with her all the time, rather than chasing all over the country trying to find the doctor."

"You couldn't have helped her that much. And besides, it isn't only a new invention, but we'd have to join the company to get it and you know we're not supposed to be unequally yoked with unbelievers."

"Sure, I know, but we can rent a phone from the company. That way we won't be yoked with unbelievers. Besides, if all of us in this township who are Amish got one we could almost have our own company."

"I doubt if you could. There'd always be some high people moving in who'd want to join the company; how could you keep them out? And besides, what about those who are living around here who've left the church? We're supposed to shun those and they'd probably want a telephone, too."

"Well, it might not work, but I still say you could rent. And I still think the telephone is a good thing and can be used to the honor and glory of God."

"How can it be?" Christ thundered. "Nothing but the devil could get a voice through a wire like that. And I want no part with the devil."

"Oh, Christ," Dan said miserably. "How can you say that? Why the thing is proved out scientifically, the batteries send impulses through the wire—I don't understand

157

all of it myself but I know it isn't the devil. It's something real simple if you hear it explained."

"Humph. Everything's scientific, scientific, nowadays. If we allow the telephone next thing we'll have the automobiles—"

"Why, why ever not? I sure would like to have one. That is, if we got roads that are good enough, or if they make one that isn't so expensive."

"See. That's just another one of those modern inventions of the devil. If we have the telephone and automobile and everything else that comes along, where is our self-denial? Where's our meek and humble spirit?"

"Oh, Christ, our meek and humble spirit can be shown even if we talk on the telephone and we can practice self-denial even if we drive an automobile."

"I'd like to know how. Why everytime I go to the city I meet one of those high and mighties who won't as much as raise their hand for a howdy, even those who used to be friendly when they drove a horse and buggy. That man who works at the mill—he's one of them. When he drove a horse and buggy he'd always wave and maybe stop and talk if he met you but last week when I was in the city I met him driving one of those newfangled devil wagons, I call them, and he didn't as much as nod his head or let on he saw me. If that isn't being lifted up with pride, I'd like to know what is."

"Oh, Christ!" Dan was helpless in the face of such scorn. How could one help Christ see that maybe the man might have been so unsure of himself behind the wheel that he dared not lift his hand from it or take his eyes from the street?

"No, Katie and I decided that if telephones are allowed we'll move down to one of the Lapland churches. In fact, I'm going to look around this summer for a farm to rent down there. Even if the telephones aren't allowed, there's too much pride creeping in anyway. The way I see it, we never should have built a church house. Ever since we did things have been going downhill."

"Why, Christ, how can you say that? Our membership is growing so much we need a larger building. We've got lots of young people joining the church and it looks as if there are more growing up."

"Oh, sure, numbers, yes. But we've got some stiff-necked people who never want to listen to the bishop. Instead of thanking God for a good one who holds true, I could name half a dozen men who wish Jacob Swartzentruber would get out. Then they could go their gainsaying newfangled way."

Again Dan was at a loss to answer. It was true that the bishop had many members under him who could perhaps show more brotherly love, but even Christ had to admit that Jacob could be a domineering man. Those who disagreed in any way came under his steely scorn and were held in suspicion. No, Jacob had never learned that some men were easily led but hard to push.

"Well, if you feel that way, there's nothing I can say, I guess," Dan said heavily, turning to go. "We've been friends, closer than brothers, all our lives. It hurts that we can't see alike on this—"

"You could see it like I do if pride weren't working in you," Christ said. He had finished sorting nails and now he picked up an old broom and began to sweep dust and shavings from his workbench.

"Pride working in me! Whatever do you mean?"

"Oh, you don't need to act as if you don't know about it. But I've noticed it. Ever since you went forward that evening in the Werey Church, pride has been growing in you. You've grown away from the old ways more and more—"

"Christ, Christ, how can you say that? If you only realized how miserable I was before, knowing I was a lost sinner on my way to hell—"

"Why, see, you're even judging yourself. And only God can judge—"

159

"And the peace I received after that, knowing Jesus Christ had died for my sins. Oh, Christ, I thought it meant something to you, too."

"Not the way you're going at it. If you wanted to stay humble and meek I could believe you, but it just goes to show something's wrong if you want to allow every devilish new thing that comes along. You can't tell me that isn't being lifted up with pride."

Dan felt as if he'd been kicked in the stomach. Slowly he started through the shop door. "If that's the way you feel, I guess there's no use trying to change your mind," he said heavily.

"No, there isn't. I'm not about to change my mind."

"Well, I guess I'll go then."

Christ didn't even look up as Dan somehow mounted his horse and took off for home over the muddy road. If Savilla guessed from his face that something was wrong she wisely said nothing and waited for him to tell her. All evening a battle raged in his heart. *You could see it like I do if pride weren't working in you. . . . You could see it like I do if pride weren't working in you. . . . Ever since you went forward that evening at the Werey Church*—Two forces seemed to be battling in his heart and brain. Mechanically he forked hay down for the horses and cows and slopped the pigs and helped Savilla with the milking. Afterward, he was unusually quiet at the supper table and while Savilla cleared off and washed the dishes. Rather than playing with Alta as he usually did, he asked for her bottle and held her quietly so that she fell asleep. He felt Savilla looking at him intently several times that evening but the turmoil within was so great that he coudn't yet speak about it.

It was several days before he had gained a measure of spiritual and mental equilibrium. Christ had said that newfangled inventions cause pride but a verse from James came into mind. "Every man is tempted when he is drawn away of his own lusts and enticed." Pride was not found in out-

160

ward things, Dan reminded himself. It was part of the makeup of the sinful human nature within every man. It could be manifested in many ways, not the least of which was one's attitude toward one's own so-called humility. He felt a deep pain as he realized that Christ's own holier-than-thou attitude toward those who disagreed with him was one of the most displeasing attitudes of all, as far as Jesus Christ was concerned. He thought of the Pharisees who harped so much on outward formalism, but who were called hypocrites, play actors if you please, by the Lord Jesus Christ. No, pride was a condition of the heart and had nothing to do with modern conveniences or newfangled inventions.

And to think that Christ felt Dan had fallen into pride ever since he had gone forward that evening at the Werey Church. That hurt. How could Christ even think such a thing? If he only knew the peace that had been Dan's since that night! No longer to bear that heavy burden of guilt and sin, but rather to know one was in right standing with a holy God because Jesus Christ had died on the cross for his sins—oh, Christ could say what he wanted to but Dan was never going back into his former state of unrest again!

Afterward, Dan could see that it had been good for him to have that talk with Christ. It made him search the Scriptures for a firm foundation and his roots had gone down deeper in faith. But it was the end of their friendship. Except for brief exchanges about the weather they seldom spoke together. Before the year was over Christ and Katie had moved to the Sharon district. Months and even years passed between seeing each other and that was usually limited to the funerals of mutual relatives. They did have one last talk, but that was years later.

14

It was downright hot, Dan thought, mopping his face with
his handkerchief. This August was true to its Midwestern
reputation—good corn-growing weather, although modern
farmers like Vernon said it was better to have cooler days
and some rain in August than the heat and humidity they'd
been having. Now when the residents of the Home came
together they reminisced of the hot days of bygone years
rather than the cold and blizzardy ones. The Home was not
centrally air-conditioned. Each resident had either a room
air-conditioner or a fan, whichever he or she could afford or
preferred, but the main lounge and dining room and office
downstairs were air-conditioned and when the individual
rooms became too unbearable the occupants fled to the
coolness of these two main rooms.

The humidity was hard on the heart patients and James
seldom left the Home, not even to take a walk around the
grounds in an evening when it cooled off. Dan, seeing his

friend's pale, calm face more than once had the feeling of looking at someone who was only a heartbeat away from the glory beyond.

As for Dan, the heat didn't bother him, except for the hottest part of the afternoon when he was out in it. Ever since his bout with pneumonia he had sought warmth as a cat does and now he sat in the sun of the morning, waiting for Judy once again. She was canning peaches that day and he had volunteered to help peel them if she came down for him. Since she said she needed sugar and jar lids anyway she was coming into town and would pick him up after she had stopped at the supermarket for her supplies.

The town was taking on the fulfilled look of the summer. Already maples were dropping a few leaves on grass turning brown from the heat. It had been two weeks since the last good rain and people were beginning to fear a dry spell. The crops still looked good, though; the cornfields surrounding the Home were in full tassel and Dan loved to come out in the evening and enjoy the undescribably delicious aroma of corn pollen.

It had been a productive year again and housewives were busy from early until late, canning and freezing the produce and fruits of the gardens and orchards of the community. He wondered if there was a kitchen in all the town that was not the scene of some such activity this week. He felt a pang of sympathy for all the busy women, especially the young mothers who were frantically working not only to preserve nature's bounty but also working against time to get their children ready for school. He remembered how Savilla had always been so harried the last few weeks of summer. Until Alta was old enough to assist Savilla, he had come into the kitchen many a time to help peel peaches or tomatoes or shuck corn for drying. It had been years since he'd last done any of it but he was sure he could still wield a paring knife; thank God his fingers weren't stiff.

Since the short dry spell had set in there was no need to

163

mow lawns; usually on a nice day all through the season one heard a lawn mower somewhere in the area, but today there were none. A bee buzzed around the asters in the flower bed in front of him and as always he heard the faint hum of life in town and on the highway west of him. In a few hours the locusts would begin their sleepy monotonous song but it was a little early in the day for them yet.

He looked toward the parking lot and the street beyond and saw Judy's little Vega drive up. He arose, lifted his cane from the seat beside him, and went down the walkway to meet her.

"I'm ready," he called, as she stopped in front of the un-loading ramp and got half out of the car.

"I see." She got in again and reached over and opened the car door for him. He climbed in and pulled it shut and then turned and smiled at her.

"Well, here we go," she said. "She was dressed in a short pant-skirt and sleeveless blouse, shirttail hanging out for comfort. She was tanned a warm brown from all her hours of gardening and lawn work, plus some "lying out," she could have told him.

"How many peaches do you have to can?" he asked.

"Two bushel, plus I've go to do something with some ap-ples. Daddy brought in a bushel of windfalls this morning— yellow transparent, the kind Mother always said made the best sauce. I don't see how she did it all. I've been tied to the kitchen for the last week and I never knew that she was."

"She would have been, though," he assured her. "I think you're doing real well, honey. Don't get discouraged."

"I really could sometimes," she admitted. They had been backing out and driving through the parking lot and the streets of the town and now they came to the highway. She pushed on the accelerator and since the windows were down because of the heat she had unconsciously raised her voice above the whistles of the wind. The shrill sound hurt

164

his ears and he winced and reached over and rolled up the window on his side.

"It is too cool for you?" she asked, slowing down momentarily.

"Oh, Judy, we old people are funny. We're always too hot or too cold."

She rolled her window up halfway. "Anyway, I've appreciated Mother more this summer than I did in all of the rest of my life together, I think. How did she keep it up? Especially when we kids were small."

"I expect it kind of grows on you."

"Daddy helps some, but he's got all of his work to do. In fact, sometimes I think he needs assistance more than I do."

"Isn't Gary at home now?"

"For about two weeks. But he's not much of a help for Daddy. I wish he would be; at least when Jim comes home he puts on his blue jeans and goes out and works but Gary doesn't. That poor kid seems to get more confused every time he goes away. I think what he needs is to ask the Lord into his heart the way I did last spring."

"Oh, Judy, I've wondered about that, too."

They were already slowing down for the turnoff of the highway and since she had to drive slower on the gravel road she rolled down her window and leaned her elbow on it. "I thought maybe he'd know what he wanted to do by now; that VS term was only for two months and now he's at loose ends again. He doesn't know what he wants to do."

"You mean he's gone through all those years of college and graduate school and still hasn't decided? I thought he wanted to be a teacher like Jim."

"I know. But teachers aren't finding it as easy to land jobs as they used to and I don't think he found what he wanted."

"All that money poured into college for him seems a waste, if he's no more decided on his lifework than that."

"I know. It's no wonder Daddy gets impatient with him."

165

She slowed down to turn into their driveway and now she pulled up to the garage. He got out and reached back to help her with the groceries. She let him take one bag and deftly took the other two and preceded him up the walk.

The house was cool inside; Vernon had installed central air-conditioning a number of years ago, and it was almost too cool for him.

"Hi, Grandpa," Gary called from the kitchen where he was eating a bowl of cereal.

"You just get up?" Dan asked. Try as he would, he couldn't keep a faint note of disapproval out of his voice.

"Best time of the day to sleep," Gary said. He was dressed in cut-off blue jeans and tank top and his brown feet were bare.

"Best time of the day to work, too," Dan said. "I always tried to get done what had to be done on a hot day like this early in the morning, then I could lie around an hour or so in the afternoon when it was too hot for the horses."

"Times have changed, Grandpa. My dear father does not even use horses but has an air-conditioned cab on his tractor. 'His brows were wet with honest sweat' doesn't apply to the 'noble workers of the soil' nowadays."

"You don't have to make fun of them. I don't see you sweating either," Judy pointed out, busy putting away groceries.

"Of course you don't. Why should I get entangled in the mesh of materialism? Farmers nowadays are so greedy for the almighty dollar it's revolting."

"The almighty dollar, I notice, came in mighty handy to pay college bills," Dan said wryly.

The boy had the grace to accept the thrust without replying. He sipped his glass of milk lazily.

"Where's your peaches, Judy?" Dan asked.

"They're down in the basement. Wait a sec and I'll go down and get a panful."

"With this strong, healthy boy sitting here?" Dan asked.

"Who, me? Sure, Jude, I can get them. Why didn't you tell me to?" He pushed back his chair and got up. "What do you want, a whole bushel up here?"

"Oh, yes, you might as well. The kitchen's cool so it won't hurt."

In a few minutes Dan was seated in front of the kitchen table with a pan on his lap full of peaches and a bigger one on the table in front of him ready to receive the peeled peach halves. After aimlessly turning on the TV controls Gary came out and lounged against the door watching him while Judy loaded the dishwasher with fruit jars.

"That looks easy, Grandpa," Gary said.

"I was just going to suggest you come over and help—unless you're too busy." The last was sarcasm but it was lost on Gary.

"Sure. Don't have anything else to do."

In a minute he, too, was installed with a pan of peaches. They worked in silence for a while, both men intent on getting the peach halves peeled with a maximum of peach left over after the peeling was removed. Dan had not helped peel peaches since the summer before Savilla died, but automatically he tried to make as thin a peel as possible. Gary, who had never peeled a peach before, found himself with a thicker peel than the small peach half that he tossed into the pan.

"You're getting the peeling too thick," Dan told him.

"Jeepers, I know! How do you get them so thin?"

"I've had some practice," Dan said wryly.

"Grandpa's probably peeled more peaches than you've ever eaten, haven't you, Grandpa?" Judy asked. She had finished with the fruit jars and now she too joined them.

"I suppose. Anyway, when I was Gary's age I used to help Savilla, your grandmother, a lot through canning season. It was lay-by time for the corn this time of year and the oats was usually threshed and it was too early to hull clover seed and we only had one crop of hay instead of all

167

that alfalfa to cut so at this time of the year most farmers had a little breathing spell."

"What'd you do then? I thought you got up early so you could work the horses while it was cool," Gary said.

"Oh, yes. Sometimes we put in fence or mowed along fencerows or caught up on odds and ends we didn't have time for earlier in the season. Sometimes we built something or went visiting. Lots of reunions were held then, too. But since Savilla was busier at that time of summer than I was, I helped her quite a lot. She wasn't always strong."

"I think it would be better if we lived like that again," Gary said. "People weren't as rushed and life must have been simpler then—not so cluttered with materialism as it is now."

"Look here, young man," Dan said tartly, a peach half pierced on his knife ready to be tossed into the waiting pan, "I wish you'd get that idea out of your head. People in every age can be obsessed with materialism. One of my neighbors, when we first got married, used to work seven days a week to earn money to buy more land; if ever a man was wrapped in materialism it was he. He died owning two sections of land but he had been so selfish that only about two dozen people attended his funeral."

"Yeah, but most people were neighborly and friendly and always ready to help someone—"

"How do you know? You weren't there to see it and I was. The truth is, some were that way and some were selfish and mean and indifferent to Jesus Christ and the plight of other people just like they are today."

"Yeah, but you didn't have so many things to buy. Madison Avenue hadn't seduced everybody yet—"

"What's Madison Avenue?"

"The advertising world. They pressure us to buy and buy and spend and spend and waste so business can sell us more and get fat with the profits."

"Oh, I'll admit that we weren't bombarded with ad-

168

vertisements the way we are now; why we didn't even get a magazine or a newspaper at home when I was little until Pa subscribed to the *Iowa Homestead* when I was about ten. Then a few years later he started getting the Davenport paper. Of course, nowadays you have radio and TV doing their share, too."

"I'll bet you didn't see all these signs advertising stuff and business putting pressure on people to buy—"

"Oh, I wouldn't say that," Dan said, his eyes twinkling. "The patent medicine companies had their ads all over even before I was born. They used to have a big sign advertising some miraculous tonic painted right on the rocks beside Niagara Falls, they tell me, until Congress passed laws that they couldn't desecrate the handiwork of nature with patent medicine signs. In fact, the patent medicine companies might have been the beginning of, what did you call it, Madison Avenue?"

"Ah, you're kidding. I thought advertising was peculiar to our age."

"Haven't you ever seen some of those faded signs on old barns in your gadding about the country?" Dan asked.

"Like, 'Chew Mail Pouch'?" Judy asked.

"Exactly! Most of those were first painted at the turn of the century or at least before the First World War. No, advertising isn't that new and neither is high-pressure salesmanship. The high-pressure salesman of my father's day were the land sharks and patent medicine chislers. By the time I was married it was some of the modern conveniences—autos, tractors, and all of that stuff."

"Yeah, but nowadays we get so much of it. You can't turn on TV or radio or open a magazine or drive through the country without being bombarded with big business, via Madison Avenue, all out to get your dollar and get fat on profit."

"I admit we get a lot more of that, especially through TV and radio, but for all your gripe against big business, as you

169

call it, I notice you like to use those products as well as the next person. You drive a modern sports car, you have a stereo, I believe Judy told me you now have a CB in your car, and you take for granted running water, the telephone, a gas-burning furnace, and all of those things I didn't even dream of at your age. How do you reconcile that attitude with your hatred of big business? Someone has to supply those things to you."

"Yeah, but that's different—" Gary protested.

"Not so's you'd notice. You couldn't even live without big business."

"Why not? You did. You lived simply and didn't have to buy much at the store."

"Oh, sure, we weren't as dependent on outside forces but still we had to have some. One of the greatest hardships of our forefathers was having to do without. Why when Daniel P. Guengerich first came here with his family in the spring of 1846 he had only the bare essentials for living and you wouldn't even be able to exist with as little as they had. Like that song we sang through the Depression, "We do not live, we only stay, we are too poor to move away!" That was their state exactly. Great-grandma was so homesick that she cried most of the time. And then as if that weren't bad enough their team of horses, their all-important means of transportation and the only source of field power to get the crops in, that team died and Great-grandpa had to trade his pocketknife to get his corn plowed. Then later on they were able to trade for some yearling calves and that was their means of transportation for years. You couldn't live like that again; you're not conditioned to it. You'd go through—through—"

"Cultural shock," Judy said.

"Yes—yes! That's it! I knew I'd heard it called that."

"That's what our English professor at EMC called it."

"And you don't think I'd survive it," Gary said, a crooked little smile on his face.

"Oh, I'm not saying you couldn't survive. But you'd have a lot different attitude than you do now."

"Missionaries do though. Some of our Pax workers are put in situations like that," Gary said.

"Yes, but they do go through cultural shock. I guess that's where I heard about it. Besides, in the back of their mind there's always the knowledge that that life is only temporary, that as soon as their term is over they can go back where all of these products of big business are available. It's not as if they were in a situation like our great-grandfather; he was in a hard, hard place and there was no way out. I tell you, that does something to you."

There was silence for a moment. Gary struggled with a peach half and even Judy was no more proficient than Dan.

"How did our great-greats stand it?" Gary asked.

"They had faith in God as a sure anchor," Dan said. "They were like the missionaries and Pax workers; they knew this life was only temporary—that when life with all its hardships was over they had a better home in heaven. They passed that on to their children and so on down the line. Each generation has to renew that faith and send it on down, or we'll lose our most precious possession."

"I can't see that my progenitor did much passing of that kind," Gary said bitterly. "All he passed on, or tried to, was faith in the almighty dollar."

"Gary! You ought to be ashamed of yourself!" Judy said. "If you knew how hard he works—and how uncomplaining he is when you want more money! You make me sick!"

"Well, all I know is he works from early morning until late in the evening so what else can I conclude? He wants me to do the same but I'll be darned if I will—"

"Gary!" Judy said again. "Now you're using language Mother used to wash our mouths out for!"

"Gary," Dan began quietly. "Your dad works those long hours because he was taught to. When he was forming his work habits we had to work that hard to get everything

171

done. You get back to that same thing we're talking about—modern conveniences. Your dad was taught to work hard, to be thrifty, to be a good steward of his earthly possessions, and as modern conveniences came along he started utilizing what he could fit into his scheme of things. One thing they probably never taught you in college, but I'd like to hammer it into your brain. It follows as inevitably as night follows day that if a person is thrifty and hardworking and a good steward of his goods, prosperity will follow. You can't get away from it, even if you want to. Now I can't look into your father's heart to see if what you accuse him of is true, but I do know one thing—your father is the product of all of his teachings. If he's got his nose to the grindstone maybe it's because my generation taught him he had to. If that's wrong then I'm partly to blame. But I might say in my defense, we had to or starve. Because we didn't have the means to do otherwise."

For a long time no one said anything. The pan of peaches began to fill and Judy got up and started filling jars. By and by it was dinnertime and Vernon came in, burned red-brown by the sun and sweaty from the heat. He greeted his father-in-law in his usual quiet way and only looked at his son without speaking. Gary refused to meet his father's eyes.

Gary did help Judy put dinner on the table; it was one of those haphazard meals women appease their men with on a busy day with a promise of better things the next meal. After the blessing had been invoked Gary took his plate of sandwiches and potato chips and pork and beans to the family room and turned on the TV. Judy ate with one eye on the cooker on the stove; the next peaches were due to come off in ten minutes, so only Dan and Vernon talked.

"What are you doing these days?" Dan asked Vernon.

"I was cutting oats stubble this morning. I think maybe I'll bale it for hay. The new seeding's about a foot high and it'd be an awful waste to let it dry up."

172

"Do you need it for hay?"

"Oh, not especially. But someone else might and then I could sell it."

"Is the third cutting alfalfa going to amount to anything if we don't get rain pretty soon!

"Oh, it won't be bad. A rain would help but we got a good soaker right after I cut it last time and it just shot up overnight, seemed like."

"Steers about ready to go?"

"Not before fall."

They lapsed into silence. Since the peaches were ready to come out of the cooker Judy got out a package of cookies and a carton of ice cream and shoved a dish of sliced peaches at them and let them help themselves. Gary came back during a commercial, loaded up his plate, and left again.

When Dan and Vernon were done Dan settled down on the couch in the dining room for a short nap and Vernon took the mail to the living room and turned on the TV there and settled in his favorite chair. Only Judy was still busy in the kitchen getting another batch of peaches ready to go into the cooker. He couldn't rest long, Dan thought sleepily. He hadn't come out to sleep. After awhile Vernon's newspaper dropped and he too dozed off.

Half an hour later they were at it again. One bushel was now disposed of and Gary went after the next one. Vernon headed back outside into the heat of the day; it was one of the hottest days yet and no sign of rain. They worked in silence at first, then Gary began to talk of his term of Voluntary Service in a camp for retarded children.

"Did you like that work?" Dan asked.

"Oh, so-so. They needed someone so I felt as if I were contributing something but I don't know if I'd have the patience to stick with it longer than just for summer camp."

"What do you like to do? Surely someday you'll decide what to do for your lifework."

"Why must I?"

"Because the Bible tells us to work with our hands so we'll have to give to those less fortunate than we are. If any will not work, let him also not eat, the Apostle Paul said. If my Pa said that once he said it a hundred times to us when we groused about work."

"Well, I know, but that's all I've ever heard. Work, work, work! We've got to work and get ahead. Work, to pay for another farm—another tractor—Is there no room in our society for the thinker or the philosopher?"

"Yes, if in the end his life is for the good of all."

"That's it!" Gary pointed his knife at him. "I want my life to be of service to humanity!"

"That's a good thing," Dan said quietly. "But how can your life be of service to humanity when you're flitting around without a purpose?"

"I've got to find what I'm here for, don't I? How can I know how my life will best serve humanity if I don't try different areas?"

"You know, Gary, man is on this earth for only one purpose—to bring honor and glory to God. Anything short of that is gypping yourself or God or humanity."

"Well, then, how can I bring honor and glory to God? I suppose by coming back here and settling down and being just like everyone else. Work for the sake of work and go to church on Sunday." His voice was bitter.

"If God should call you back here, yes. But the very starting point of bringing glory to God is first making a personal commitment to the Lord Jesus Christ and confessing Him as our Lord and Savior from sin."

"That's Holy Roller stuff."

"Is it? Then I've been a Holy Roller all these years."

"And I just became one last spring," Judy put in. "But if that's Holy Roller stuff it's the best thing I ever did. At least now I've got something to cling to." Gary gave her a quick glance.

174

"And Gary, this bothers me—you saying what you did about wanting your life to be of service to humanity. What makes you think that someone like your father isn't serving humanity?"

"Dad? A farmer making money hand over fist? You call that a service to humanity?" Gary looked at him incredulously.

"I'm not talking about the money. I'm thinking of something you take for granted so much that it doesn't even enter your thinking. I'm thinking of all of the millions of people in the world wanting what the farmer produces and the most elemental of physical needs. Food. What makes you think that producing all that good beef and ham and bacon and soybeans isn't doing a service to humanity?"

Gary paused in the act of peeling a peach half, opened his mouth as if to speak, closed it again, and went right on peeling.

"Why, boy," Dan continued in a much softer voice, "you can be of service to humanity by just running a gas station."

Judy looked up quickly, glanced from Dan to Gary, then went on peeling also.

"I remember one time when Savilla and I, your grandmother, you know, when she and I went on a trip. After I was working at the mill, we went on a trip down through Kentucky and Tennessee and southern Ohio to see Alta who was living there at the time. Anyhow, on our way home we drove until late—Savilla wanted to stop early but I didn't. I should have listened to her but that's too late now. Anyway, I kept on driving and driving and it got late and we were in the middle of southern Indiana and all at once the generator light came on. We only had a mile to the next town, thank God, and our lights got dimmer and dimmer.

"Well, when we finally got to town—it was about the size of ours here—there was only one gas station that could help us and that man was just ready to lock up. But he was good-natured enough to help us out and call up the fellow who

175

sold auto parts and between the three of us it was eleven-thirty when we got it done. Then the man called the only hotel in town and, thank goodness, we could go to bed and sleep for the night. Now if that man wasn't doing a service to humanity I'd like to know who was. Just supplying the goods and services needed by people is doing a service to humanity."

Again Gary paused in the act of peeling peaches, gave him a long searching look, and seemed about to say something. Then he shook his head a little and went back to peeling peaches.

15

The town was crowded with tourists. In the past few years the most prominent businessmen of the community had begun to devise means of enticing tourists to the area to view the Old Order people in their familiar setting. It had been done in the East for several decades so why not here? At first it had been only a trickle hardly worth noticing, from Cedar Rapids, from the Quad Cities along the Mississippi, then from Des Moines and farther west, until now one saw big tour buses in town almost every week. Most of them were women's groups, although on Saturdays there were also families, and tour guiding was an established profession.

There had long been a historical society among the Mennonite groups and now even they began to cater to the tourist. The town and the society had turned some vacant weed-infested lots along one of the highways into a historical village, adding a schoolhouse, a railroad depot, a grandpa house, and so on as the funds were available until now it was a sizable attraction, along with the Mennonite Historical Archives and a community museum. Only the Old Order drew away in contempt and refused to have anything to do with it. When a curious tourist pointed at them the Old Order turned their faces away or hid them in the confines of a bonnet or broadbrimmed straw hat. Of the whole community, the Old Order were the greatest tourist attraction, but the least inclined to take part in the tourist trade, preferring to be left to live their lives in peace.

Now the community was having its annual fall festival. That was why it was so crowded with tourists that it was hard to find a parking space downtown. It was a two-day festival and since this town of over a thousand people had only one small hotel and had never boasted a motel, out-of-town visitors either had to go to the city or make only a one-day stay. Many who had grown up in the area, but now lived in other communities, stayed with their relatives or friends.

There was to be a hymn sing on the evening of the first day, along with special music from most of the churches in the area. Dan was waiting for Judy to come after him for that. There had been a shuttle bus between the Home and the historical grounds all afternoon and he could have gone with one of those loads but Judy had wanted him to wait for her. She had grapes to can during the day and couldn't get away before evening.

Luckily, the weather was mild, Dan thought. But even so, he had his coat lying across his lap as he waited in the lounge. He saw John Schlabach coming toward him like a worm inching its way along; John was getting too crippled and frail to leave the Home anymore. For a moment, Dan felt grateful that the Lord had so far given him a good measure of health and strength. At eighty-seven one could so easily be much worse. The thought made him especially patient with John.

"You going out?" John asked. Although his legs were feeble, his voice wasn't.

"Judy's going to take me down to the festival."

"The what?" John cupped his ear.

"The festival. Down at the historical grounds."

"Oh." John inched his way to a position in front of the chair, then slowly lowered himself into it. "Is it worth going?"

"Oh, I think so. Didn't you talk with any of those who were down there this afternoon? Mandy Swartzentruber said it was interesting."

"What?"

"Mandy Swartzentruber said it was interesting."

"Oh." John adjusted his cane across the chair arm. "What they got to see?"

"Oh, all kind of things. They got that new bake oven, Mandy says. They bake bread in it and sell it and they cook cider *lodviek*—"

"Cook what?"

"Cider lodviek."

"Never did like that stuff." John snorted. "Give me grape jelly any day. Why I remember Ma used to cook cider lodviek and we all had to help—maybe that's why I hate the stuff—and we had to take turns standing there and stir and stir and stir. It'd take us all day. And sometimes Ma would get tired of cooking it herself and she'd throw in some squash so it would get thick quicker. Oh, we'd eat it— nothing better to eat, I guess. But I sure didn't like it."

"So? Well, anyway, Mandy says they're pressing cider and cooking lodviek and making soap and grinding corn-meal—anything that we used to have to do in the old days."

"Yah, and the young generation, they think they'd like to go back to doing things like that again—phooey! They'd last about one day and then they'd be glad to come back to modern life."

"Could be, splitting wood or shucking corn by hand—"

179

"Yah! Or stacking loose hay on a wagon or stumbling behind a walking plow all day. Or just plain good hard sweating! The way people act, there's a law against that!"

"Against what?"

"Sweating!"

"Oh? Well we never liked it either."

"What?"

"I said we never liked it either."

"Maybe not, but we did it. We had to or perish. We couldn't sit in an air-conditioned tractor cab and plow corn—we had to walk shanks' mare behind the horses."

"And if it was too hot we quit because it was too hard on the horses." Dan's eyes twinkled. "Never mind us."

"Yah. That's the truth."

He thought of that afterward when he and Judy were making their way among the crowds clustered around the various exhibits. The cider press and the burr mill and the lodviek cooking and soapmaking had shut down for the evening and the last batch of bread had been taken out of the big old-fashioned outdoor oven just before they got to it. But the results of the various projects were still on sale at the booths. Judy bought a loaf of bread and a jar of lodviek for breakfast the next morning.

Afterward they gathered for the program. Dan was glad for his coat now even though he hadn't needed it as long as the sun was shining. Someone's flatbed trailer had been pulled in front of the historical building for use as a platform, and chairs were arranged in a semicircle in front of it, as far as the open space allowed. But those were soon full and latecomers sat on the grass or stood if they were afraid of the cool ground.

Each church of the area was represented except the Old Order, and as Dan watched and listened he could not help seeing the participants' parents or grandparents, if he had known them, like an invisible array of spectators. A verse from the Book of Hebrews came to mind: "Wherefore seeing we also are compassed about with so great a cloud of witnesses. . . ."

What would they think of us, he thought, those old ones who worked so hard to build this into a solid community of faith? And yet, their opinion was not the highest or the one that counted most. "What does the Lord think of us," he wondered. "Did our fathers build right? Did those of my generation pass on our faith so that our children can pass that glorious, wonderful, life-giving faith on to their children?" Ah, he hoped so! "Don't ever let this community be without Thy witness, Lord," he prayed.

One group represented a non-Mennonite church in the Sharon area with the yet familiar Mennonite names of Miller and Yoder and Stutzman and Kinsinger and he felt a dull pain as he listened to them sing. This had been one of the tragedies of all of those hair splits and personality clashes of two generations ago, he knew. When the traditions of men are forced on any church to the exclusion of the gospel it can only result in complete abandonment of restrictions of any kind and this had happened at the time this particular congregation had been formed. Many of their best members had come from the Old Order in the Sharon district.

It grew cool toward the last and he wished he could stand it better. "Are you getting cold, Grandpa?" Judy whispered as she saw him draw his coat closer about him.

He nodded.

"Why don't we go then?" she asked in a low voice. "If we go now we'll get out of here before the rush begins. Besides, I don't want you getting pneumonia again."

"But I didn't see everything I wanted to see," he told her later, as she drove slowly through the parked cars along the highway.

"I can take you down tomorrow," she said. "I can come in the morning and take you down and come back and get you later on."

181

"Oh, that's not necessary. I can go down with a load from the Home. Today they were going back and forth all of the time."

"You're sure?"

"Yes. Of course if you wanted to come down anyhow, I'll wait on you."

"Well, our MYF is running a booth and I said I'd help tomorrow afternoon so—"

"Why, that would work out fine. I can go down toward noon with a load from the Home and then you can take me back."

So it was decided and the next day he was mingling with the crowds again. There were so many to visit with. A few were older than he, but many were ten or twenty years younger, persons he had known all of their lives; often he'd known their fathers and even grandfathers. If there was anyone in the area he might not have known otherwise, his years of working at the mill had acquainted him with those. He had almost become an institution although he did not know it.

It had been quite some time since he had been in the historical building and he spent a long time looking. It might have gone faster if he had not found so many to visit with, he thought with amusement. Here was a display of old Bibles, old German songbooks, old valentines, and right beside was an old pie safe such as his mother had had in the kitchen. Further on was an old phonograph such as he and Savilla had bought in 1927, just before the crash. It was like meeting old and forgotten friends, some well liked and some disliked.

He turned a corner and was in a kitchen display. All at once he was back in the kitchen of the farm and it was evening and just such a teakettle was singing on a kitchen range exactly like this one—a cheerful homey sound he had always loved, the teakettle singing and maybe the fire crackling, and the room fragrant with the smell of newly

182

baked bread or pies or cookies. Almost it seemed as if Savilla should come out of the pantry with a pitcher of milk or a plate of butter.

For a long while he stood there, a little to the side so others could see, looking as if he could not get enough. Long before they moved to town he had bought Savilla a new bottled-gas stove. The old wood range had been scrapped and at the time he'd had no regrets; in fact he'd been glad he no longer needed to split wood. But now he could feel the pleasant warmth of the fire on a cold winter evening just as plainly as if he were once more warming his hands over it while he waited for Savilla to dish up supper.

After a moment he became aware of someone else who had been looking for a while—a young woman a little older than Judy, dressed in blue jeans and chambray shirt with a blue denim jacket over her shirt. He looked up and met her eyes and smiled.

"It looks so peaceful," she said wistfully.

"Yes, it does."

"Tell me, you must have grown up—you must have had one like this at one time. Was it as peaceful as it looks?"

"It was for me," he said, the memory of those long-ago evenings vivid in his mind.

"It would be nice if it were still—I mean, somehow it seems as if life was simpler then. There weren't all of the hard questions to answer—"

"Child, child," he chided gently. "Don't get that idea in your head. It was peaceful for me because I had inward peace. But as far as hard questions to answer—I—we had them, too." He thought suddenly of Christ.

"You mean even in those days there were complexities and—and—hard things?"

"Yes, there were. What makes you think there weren't?"

"Oh, I don't know. Maybe it was hearing my grandmother talk about the olden days. It always sounded so good and I thought—" Her voice trailed off.

"We old people forget the hard things. Maybe it's just as well. When you get to my age a lot of your life is memories and no one likes an unpleasant situation. I guess we forget the bad things so we can stand to keep on living."

She met his eyes again and smiled shyly.

"Are you from around here?" he asked.

"I live here now, but I was raised in Pennsylvania. My husband grew up around here."

"Oh, who is he? My name's Dan Brenneman, by the way."

She told him her husband's name and his parents' names, and he nodded.

"You probably knew his great-grandfathers." She smiled.

"Yes, I did, but not too well. Some of them helped start the Werey Church."

"The Werey Church?" She puckered her eyebrows.

"Now known as East Union. Only old-timers like me still remember that old name."

"Oh." She nodded and stood for a minute, her eyes still on the scene before them. Then she met his eyes again and smiled shyly once more before she drifted on.

16

Daddy and I had a letter from Jim today," Judy said. They were sitting in a booth in a steak house in the city, waiting for their steaks to be broiled. Judy had already eaten her tossed salad but Dan was still chewing his. False teeth weren't always cooperative when one ate lettuce, he had found out long ago.

"So? What does he say?"

"He found a girl." Judy giggled. "I'd given up on him. I thought he'd be a bachelor for sure."

"Your mother told me one time, though, that he wanted his education behind him before he got married. Who is she?"

"Her name is Carol Lane and her father's one of the professors at the university in Columbia. That's all he said about her."

Their number was called for steaks and Judy went to the grill to get them. While she was gone Dan watched the people around him; people-watching was still one of his favorite pastimes. Judy had asked him to come up with her for one last meal together before winter set in. The weather was still mild now in the beginning of October, but one never knew how long it would last. Ever since that spell of pneumonia last winter he had loved warmth like a cat. Unexpected drafts made him shiver and draw his coat around him even on such a mild evening as this. That was why they had chosen this booth way over in the farthest corner away from the door.

"Here's yours." She handed him a tray. "I'll get mine."

She returned with the other tray. "I hope you can chew it," she said, glancing at him as he pushed his half-eaten salad aside and took up his steak knife.

"If I go slow I usually have no trouble."

They were silent for a few moments as they began to eat.

"If you have heard that Jim has a girlfriend, what have you heard from Gary?" Dan asked after awhile.

"Not much. He lets us know he's alive and that's about all."

"So he signed up for another term of VS?"

"Yes. At that school for retarded children in Colorado."

"What does your father say?"

"Nothing. What should he say? Gary is his own boss. Besides, Daddy's so quiet. You never know what he's thinking. How did he and Mother communicate? I never noticed any lack of it when she was still here."

He thought of Savilla. She had never been talkative and yet she had never seemed quiet.

"Some people can communicate without words. Your grandmother was like that."

"Was she? Well, Daddy and Mother must have been, too. I never thought our house was quiet. Peaceful, yes, but never that kind of quiet when—well—that seems dead."

"How is your father?"

"Daddy?" She looked at him in surprise. "Oh, he's all

right—physically at least. He never complains and he works as hard as usual. So I guess he's all right."

"So?"

"But I never know about him otherwise. Grandpa—" She laid down her knife and fork and looked at him earnestly. "Did Daddy ever make a personal commitment to the Lord?"

"I don't know. I certainly hope so. Judy, I say this to my shame, but I never asked!"

"Yes, but surely he went forward before he was baptized—"

"I don't know. He was a member of East Union before he and Helen got married and he transferred his membership to Lower Deer Creek afterward. I guess I never questioned because I took it for granted that he had made a personal commitment. His life was always exemplary. But why do you ask?"

"Because all of these years I never saw Daddy read his Bible voluntarily, until this past summer."

"You mean not even for morning devotions?"

"Oh, I don't mean that. Of course, we always followed the Sunday school devotional supplement. Daddy would read that and Mother would read the Scripture references. But to sit down and pick up a Bible in the evening, no, I never saw him do it before." Her voice was grave.

"And you say he's doing it now?"

"Yes. At first I didn't give it much thought when I saw his Bible lying on that little lamp table beside his chair. I guess I thought he might have been looking at the Sunday school lesson. Even if I put it on the bookshelf where he had always kept it—the next morning it was on the table again. Now it's always lying there. And most of the time it's open," she finished simply.

Dan felt a strange lump in his throat. How much one took for granted, he thought, a sharp pain going through him. As long as one played the game according to the accepted rules one never questioned the motives. And only a discerning mind like Judy's would even notice.

"Judy, I can only say I'm sorry I never asked him. But I'm glad he's beginning to now."

"So am I," she said. "Maybe I can talk to him about the Bible and the Lord Jesus now. Outside of you and my Bible study group, there aren't many I can talk with. Sometimes I get so hungry!"

"Well, Judy, surely there are plenty of people in our church who will talk about the Lord. I have never felt a lack."

"Maybe it's me then. But you're of the older generation, Grandpa. More of those have probably made a personal commitment. But some of the people my age—or maybe a little older—say five or ten years—some of them, when you mention the name of Jesus outside a Sunday school class—they act as if you had horns in your head."

He laid down his knife and fork. The lump had come back in his throat and it felt larger than ever.

"I used to be such good friends with Susan Miller before she married Steve Yoder." Judy cut off a piece of meat. "We used to talk of everything together. But when I try to talk to her about the Lord she can't wait to change the subject."

"Oh, Judy!"

"She invited me to her house for a wiener roast last week—she had a bunch of us old friends in for Steve's birthday—and I never want to go to a party like that again. Of all the filthy stories—and they're all members of our church. And last summer they missed Sunday services for six weeks, at least. I think they went boating or camping every Sunday. It might not be so bad but she makes her mother believe they go to church regularly. I don't know how she'd pull it off if her parents went to the same church." Although she had off cut a piece of meat she only pushed it around on her plate.

"You sound like Lonnie Yoder," was all he could think of saying.

"Do I? Yes, I guess I do. But when he talked to me I couldn't have seen anything wrong with such a life. Maybe I'm a square now for even questioning it. But surely, Grandpa, being a Christian is more than calling yourself a Mennonite."

"Much more."

"Then why don't our people act like it? It's no wonder so many of the kids are going to other denominations—or quitting church altogether."

What could he say to that? She began to eat again in a halfhearted way and he poked around in his baked potato.

"We do have good preachers though," he said after awhile.

"Oh, they preach Christian living, I agree. But I don't know when I've heard any of them preach a salvation sermon. Grandpa, maybe that's one of the reasons a lot of kids my age haven't ever made a personal commitment to the Lord—maybe we never heard that we had to."

"Oh, Judy, I hope you can't say that with truth about our denomination."

"Well, when do we hear it? We hear about nonresistance and VS and loving our neighbors but when are we told about needing a Savior?"

"Then you think Lonnie was right in what he said about Mennonites?"

She laid down her fork again and met his eyes. "Oh, what can I say? He was right in some things, yes. But it hurts so much to have to admit such things about our people!" She shoved her plate aside and buried her face in her elbow on the table. He reached over painfully and patted her arm.

She raised her head again and opened her bag for a Kleenex and blew her nose. "But I thank the Lord for people in our church like you, Grandpa." She gave him a tremulous smile. "You dear old people who love the Lord are an inspiration to me. I'm so glad the Lord let you live long enough for me to talk to you like this. Especially since Mother died."

"Thank you," he said simply. "I must also say this, Judy, I'm encouraged about our denomination when I see young people like you concerned about it."

"Why, bless your heart, Grandpa," she said, smiling.

They both went back to eating, although their steaks were getting cold. "Do you ever hear from Lonnie?" Dan asked.

She shook her head. "Not since that last time he was here."

"Oh? It was a complete break then?"

"I guess so. Oh, for a long time it hurt even to think about him. But lately I kind of wish I could see him and thank him for what he said to me that day. He shook my world like an earthquake but I can see now that it was good for me."

"I'm glad you can look at it that way. But I had hoped—" he broke off.

"You'd hoped we'd get married?" She grinned.

"Well—yes, I suppose I did. I think you'd make a good wife and mother. You're a little like Savilla, your grandmother, and she was the best. I'd hate to see those talents go to waste in you."

"That's nice of you to say so, Grandpa. I can't deny that I wouldn't mind having a husband and family—if that's in the Lord's plan for me. Right now I'm willing to wait until Mr. Right comes along. But I can tell you, it will have to be one who shares my faith in Jesus Christ."

"That's the best way. Build your life on Jesus as revealed in the Scriptures and you'll have something solid."

17

The rain was beating against his window and a crack of thunder reverberated overhead. All morning the clouds had been lowering and a few minutes ago the first drops began falling, although thunder had been rumbling for the last half hour. The farmers wouldn't like this, he thought, a big rain in the beginning of November, right in the middle of corn harvest. He wondered how far along Vernon was with the harvest; he hadn't seen either Judy or Vernon for over a week. Last Sunday he had not gone out to church and it was doubtful if he would again until next spring. "If the Lord tarries or I live that long," he thought. And unless they came in to see him he might as well be a thousand miles away, for all he found out about them.

The Home was like a world in itself. He could not say it was a world apart; the residents kept up with outside happenings through radio and TV, newspapers and magazines, as well as letters or just plain gossip. It was strange how nothing that went on outside the Home ever missed mention inside, whether it was the latest marriage or a business failure on Main Street. Somehow the residents heard of it and discussed it, the ladies over quilt piecing or fancywork and the men over their checkerboards.

Right now one of the chief topics of conversation was the high. price of land. Land had always brought premium prices in the settlement, especially in the Old Order neighborhoods. Horses and buggies were confining; five miles was far enough for most of them to want to be away from town or church meetings and ten miles was such a great distance that only the young and hardy managed persistently. Others stayed at home or hired someone with a car to haul them. Consequently farms within a radius of five miles to town were in top demand. As the people multiplied, land became even more valuable until it now brought over a thousand dollars an acre. This never failed to fascinate the old-timers at the Home. How could a young man with a family to support ever pay off high-priced land like that, they argued among themselves. Suppose the bottom dropped out as in the thirties? Or the nineties before that? Only a few asked the last question, though, and then it was mostly because they had heard their fathers talk of it.

Another crack of thunder brought him back to the present. He got up and went to the window and peered out. There wasn't much to see; the rain was coming so hard that he couldn't see through the window and he turned away from it. What could he do? In the afternoon, the bulletin board said, there would be a travel film and he always enjoyed those. But right now he had no new reading matter. He had written letters to the children yesterday so that didn't nag him. Almost he envied the women with their endless quilt-piecing and fancywork for their children or grandchildren—at least it gave them something to do. He prowled around his room, poking at a pile of magazines with his cane and taking out several books and putting them back after a casual glance through them. Fannie May hadn't been in yet to dust and clean; she must be taking the other end of the hall first today.

He could go down to the lounge and watch TV but few of the daytime programs interested him enough to make the effort. Or he could go over to John Schlabach's room but John's hearing was getting so bad it was almost impossible to carry on a decent conversation. James had been moved over to the nursing section; his heart was getting so bad that he had to stay in bed all of the time now. It was a wonder he was still living.

Why did God keep all of them here on this earth anyway, he thought in a rare burst of discouragement. John with his deafness, James and his poor ailing heart, Newt so crippled with arthritis that it was like watching a worm as he slowly inched his way around the building. And his own lungs were playing out on him so that any cold air made him cough and sneeze. Why didn't God take them all to glory? What was the use of their cumbering the earth and burdening the younger generation with their aches and whining and endless memories of days gone by that interested no one but themselves?

So many of his contemporaries were gone; nine out of ten that he had grown up with had gone to their eternal destiny and those who were left weren't even the ones he'd been most compatible with a generation ago. He and John, for instance, had gone to the same country school and joined church the same time but they'd never been close. Now John was one of the few persons left of his age.

So many of his dear ones were gone—Savilla, Helen, Ma, Pa, Jacob, Lydie, and the others of his family. He was suddenly acutely homesick to see them. "Let it be soon," he prayed. "I'm ready to go, dear Lord, anytime You call."

The squeak of the cleaning cart in the hall brought him out of his reverie. A moment later Fannie May appeared at the door.

"Cleaning time?" he asked her.

"Yeah." She came in with dust mop in hand.

"I've been real dirty," he told her. "I cleaned out my desk drawer yesterday and the wastebasket overflowed."

"So?" Clearly she was not her usual cheerful self today. He peered at her closely. A simple statement like this would ordinarily have given her a fit of giggles.

"What's troubling you?" he asked. "Aren't you feeling well?"

She dropped in a chair and propped the mop against the wall. "I'm good and mad, that's what."

"Why, Fannie May, whatever for? Is it anything I've done?"

"Oh, Dan, of course not. But I'm getting so sick and tired of our preachers!"

"So?" He didn't want to question her further; she could get into more trouble with the preachers of her church if they found out she was telling tales out of school. But he need not have bothered his conscience; Fannie May was loaded and ready to unburden on anyone who gave her a kind word.

"I'm really burned up! They've been bothering poor Anna Sue ever since she joined church, about her dresses or her hair or her covering or her shoes. Her dress is too short, her hair too *strubblich*, her stockings too thin. You name it and they were hounding her. Last night was the last straw!"

"What happened last night?"

"They came over and told her, and me too, that if we didn't get those things taken care of they wouldn't let us go along to communion!"

He could see that this was a serious ultimatum. Up until a generation ago even his own church had used this method to bring recalcitrant members to heel.

"That's too bad," he said seriously.

"Well, I'm afraid it's too bad for them. Anna Sue and I have made up our minds that we're not taking anymore.

Now if we'd been doing anything that the Bible really calls sin it would be different. But if someone does anything like that they don't do a thing with them—"

"Oh, but they must!"

"No they don't. Why I know for a fact that some of the young people have been sleeping together on dates. And some of those boys get drunk at singings! And they get in fights! But do they do anything to those? Of course not! Their parents are some of the leading people in church, so they let them run and come pick on poor Anna Sue, who tries to live a decent life." She almost ran out of breath.

"That's too bad," he agreed.

"I know it! Anna Sue and I talked about it after the preachers left and we decided that we're not going to take it anymore—" She paused dramatically.

"What will you do?"

"We're going to leave the church. Anna Sue's boyfriend has been wanting her to for over a year, she said, but he put it off when he started going with her. Now they're both leaving."

"And you are, too?"

"Yes. I'd have been content to stay if they hadn't begun picking on Anna Sue so badly—and then they started on me!"

"What does your mother say?"

"She wishes we didn't have to leave but even she said she didn't blame us."

"What church are you joining?"

Fannie May named it. It wasn't the same denomination as his but many of the Old Order had joined there in the past two decades; Fannie May and her sister would find plenty of contemporaries.

"Fannie May, church membership is all well and good and I'm not saying you don't have good reason for your feelings, but you know there's something much more important than church membership, don't you?"

"What's that?"

"Making a personal commitment to the Lord Jesus Christ. Repenting of your sinful nature and asking Him to live in your heart."

She looked at him in silence for a moment. "But didn't I do that when I was baptized?"

"I don't know. I hope you did, but only you and God can answer that."

"Why I thought that if you were baptized and joined the church that was when you made your commitment."

"This would be the ideal situation, yes. I don't doubt that the commitment does come at that time for some. But not always. It didn't for me."

"You mean when you were baptized you weren't—"

"I wasn't right with God, no. I say it to my shame."

"Then why did you join?"

"To please my girl friend, and her parents. Mine were both dead or they would have been one more reason."

"Well, but when did you make this—what did you call it?—personal commitment to Jesus Christ?"

"A few years later. Praise the Lord, He convicted me of my sins so much that I had to do something. Then the Werey Church had evangelistic meetings one fall and I went forward there. After that I never doubted but that Jesus had made me right with God."

She was silent again for a moment. "You mean that's what I should do, go forward at a meeting?"

"No, not necessarily. You could do it right now in this room if you wanted to. If you know you never have before."

"I don't know how."

For a fleeting moment he thought of Judy. "You can talk to the Lord Jesus just as if He were in this room. You can tell Him, Jesus, I know I have a sinful nature and I'm sorry. But please forgive me and come into my heart and make me Yours."

For a long moment they looked at each other. Then she

196

dropped her eyes and covered her face with her hands. The silence in the room was broken by a sob. He reached over and touched her shoulder.

"God bless you, Fannie May."

° ° °

He had left her then and gone downstairs. Experience had taught him that she might need two or three reminders to get to work if she had someone to talk to and he decided it was better if he left. Newt had inched his way to the lounge and, along with some of the other male residents, was watching cartoons on TV. Only a few glanced up as Dan joined them and he made no effort at conversation as he seated himself a little to the edge of the group.

He gave a cursory glance at the cartoons but lost himself in his own thoughts almost at once. He was more moved over the last half hour than he had thought he would be. His eyes were still moist. He took out his handkerchief and wiped it across his eyes and blew his nose.

How often could Fannie May's story be multiplied across the country? How many people had equated baptism and church membership with right standing with God? How many of his own people for that matter? Such a heavy burden came over him that he wished he were back in the privacy of his room where he could close the door and cry out to God for blind eyes to be opened. Part of a verse from Jeremiah came to mind, "Oh that . . . mine eyes [were] a fountain of tears, that I might weep . . . for . . . my people."

The sound of the TV was a meaningless babble and after awhile he couldn't stand it any longer. He got up again without speaking to anyone and wandered to the window. The thunderstorm had settled into a steady downpour and the world looked gloomy and drab. It had not been as colorful this fall as last year and now the rain was making things look drearier than usual. He turned from the window and decided to go to his room again; surely Fannie May was finished by now.

197

She was, he found when he got upstairs, although her cart was outside the room next to his. He half closed the door and sank into his rocking chair.

Fannie May's case made him think of the Old Order. He had not had close contact with them for years. True, he knew most of them—or at least the men who were thirty-five or older—from his years of working at the feed mill. But after the telephone split, when the Deer Creek churches had affiliated with the different conferences, all church fellowship had broken off with the Old Order; what fellowship there was had been strictly on a secular basis. Funerals and reunions still brought them together but outside of that it was as if they were worlds apart. Consequently, it had been years since he had known any of them as personally as Fannie May, if one could call their daily encounters at the Home personal.

The last person of the Old Order to talk with him on spiritual matters had been his cousin, Christ. And that talk had been so painful that he had tried to forget it. He had not consciously thought of it for years but now the events of that day came back.

It had been a slack day at the mill, a beautiful day in late spring when farmers were too busy to come to town for feed. But at that time Christ had already turned his farm over to Samuel, his son, and he and Katie had built themselves a grandpa house in the same yard. Probably Samuel had asked his father to come to town for a load of feed since he himself was too busy planting corn to come.

Anyway, Christ had arrived at the mill with his team and his high-wheeled Charter Oak wagon. As was customary, Dan had taken him out back to the warehouse and helped him load it. Dan couldn't even remember for sure how the conversation had started but he did vaguely remember that Christ had been courteous enough as long as they stuck with talk of the weather and spring planting and such. Had Dan said something about rubber tractor tires? It could well

198

have been since the Old Order were in a ferment at one time because so many of the younger farmers favored them while the others like Christ were just as bitterly opposed to them, claiming they were modern inventions and therefore worldly and sinful. Although their members were forbidden to tell their church troubles abroad, invariably the general community got wind of the Old Order upheavals and this rubber disagreement had been no exception.

One congregation had split off the Old Order a generation ago on that very issue, a congregation immediately dubbed the rubber church by scornful Old Order people and many of the Mennonites had been so delighted with the wit that the congregation had been called that unofficially for years.

It was inevitable that he should hear much of this at the mill where garrulous old men stopped at the office to gossip every day, and he must have opened the conversation himself. Perhaps he had brought all the pain of that talk on himself. But he might never have found out Christ's true feelings if he hadn't talked with him that day.

They had already tossed on about half a wagonload of bags and they had paused for a brief rest. It was then that he had made the opening remark; it could well have been a direct question as to why the Old Order did not allow rubber tires on the tractors since steel-lugged wheels posed almost insurmountable problems, especially to those who lived on macadam roads where lugs were prohibited because they broke up the roadbed. But all at once Christ was stern.

"Shall we allow the church to follow the same road you've been on for the last thirty years?" he asked sharply.

"What road?"

"Why running after everything the world has. First it was telephones, then cars and electricity, and then radios and now even TV. There's no end to it."

"What's wrong with those things?" Dan asked in

199

genuine astonishment. "They can be used to the glory of God."

"Where's your self-denial?" Christ asked. "Everything you want you get. How can God be pleased with you? It's a wonder He doesn't send down fire from heaven and destroy you all."

"Why Christ—"

"There's five or six Mennonite churches in this community and I don't see how God can be pleased with a single one of them," Christ went on relentlessly. "And now the women are cutting their hair and not wearing the covering— Why I couldn't sleep nights if I were in your shoes."

"Christ, it's my right standing with God. That's all-important, not those things," Dan said.

"Oh my, how can you say that?" Plainly he thought Dan had uttered the worst kind of blasphemy.

"My right standing with God depends on my faith in what Jesus Christ did for me on the cross. Romans 5:1 says, 'Therefore being justified by faith, we have peace with God through our Lord Jesus Christ.'"

"You mean you're going so far as to say you're right with God?" There couldn't have been more horror in Christ's tone.

"I don't say it, the Bible does. And if the Bible says so, why can't I believe it?"

"What would be the use of the day of judgment if we could know we're right with God now?"

"God has His own purpose in judgment and it's not for me to question it; I only know that He also tells me in John that 'He that . . . believeth . . . shall not come into condemnation; but is passed from death unto life.'"

"That's blasphemy!" Christ said incredulously. "Does your church actually teach that? That's saying that you're good enough to go to heaven as you are; that teaching is eternal security and it's damned from the pit of hell—"

"No, no, Christ, I'm not saying that at all. I know that

200

I'm a poor, weak sinner and I need more than my own strength to make me right with God. All I can plead is the blood of Jesus Christ—if it weren't for that precious sacrifice on the cross there would be no hope for me."

Christ turned and began tossing feed bags onto the wagon as if the devil were after him. Plainly he wanted nothing to do with such blasphemy. Dan also turned and tossed bags to him from the back of the warehouse as fast as Christ could load them on the wagon. They must have been a sight—two old men tossing fifty-pound feed sacks as easily as if they were bean bags and all the while Dan was desperately trying to explain the gospel to his cousin.

"It says in Romans 8:1, 'There is therefore now no condemnation to them which are in Christ Jesus, who walk not after the flesh, but after the Spirit. For the law of the Spirit of life in Christ Jesus hath made me free from the law of sin and death.' And Romans 10:4 says, 'For Christ is the end of the law for righteousness to every one that believeth.' And verses 9 and 10, some of my favorites, by the way, tell us, 'That if thou shalt confess with thy mouth the Lord Jesus, and shalt believe in thine heart that God hath raised him from the dead, thou shalt be saved. For with the heart man believeth unto righteousness; and with the mouth confession is made unto salvation.' And the eleventh verse says, 'Whosoever believeth on him shall not be ashamed.' "

He paused for breath. The wagon was full anyway. Christ also took several deep breaths and mopped his face with his handkerchief and blew his nose loudly before he attempted to speak.

"If your church teaches that, it's no wonder you allow any new devil's invention that comes along. What difference does it make to you if the Bible says, 'Be not conformed to this world'? You're right with God so you can have radios and TV and cars and all the other things of the world—just as long as you have faith, faith, faith," he mimicked. "Well, I happen to know the Bible says that faith without works is dead."

"Of course it is. I never said it wasn't. But true faith will result in entirely different works than the things you mentioned." Dan urged.

Christ jumped down from the loading dock and went around to the front of the wagon and scrambled over the wheels onto the seat. He unwrapped the lines from around the front stem and gathered them in his hands. The horses, tired of standing, began to walk ahead without urging. Dan jumped off the loading dock, ran to the front of the wagon, and looked up earnestly at the other man. "Christ, please listen," he entreated. "I'm not saying anything that isn't in the Bible. Read it for yourself and see if what I quoted isn't there."

"There's danger in reading too much in the Bible." Christ frowned. "It leads away from the *Audnung*. That's another thing about your church. I guess you think you're pretty good because you study the Bible and have prayer meetings and all such stuff. So you think you can allow all of the fashions and inventions of the world because you read the Bible."

"No, no, it isn't that way at all," Dan protested.

"Giddap," Christ clucked to the horses, ignoring Dan. "Giddap." The horses pricked their ears and broke into a fast walk toward the street, Christ sitting ramrod straight on the high seat and never once looking back. Dan stood in the lot and watched him go, too stunned to talk.

It was the last conversation they ever had. Six months later Christ died of a stroke. Even though their final meeting had been so heartbreaking Dan went to the funeral. It was the last chance he would have to pay his respects to the memory of what the two of them had once shared.

18

Christmas was fast approaching again. Dan, who seemed to be living in the past more and more this past year, couldn't help remembering all the Christmases in bygone years, especially when he and Savilla had been happy together as young parents, with the children still at home. Even through the Depression, with Alta in college, they had always had enough to share with those less fortunate, even if it was no more than a fresh squash pie to an ailing neighbor or sorghum molasses cookies and homemade stuffed toys for the neighbor up the road who had a large family and poor management. Savilla might sit up until after midnight to make Helen new doll clothes from feed bag scraps or he might work out in the shop in the evenings with cold fingers to make a miniature farm wagon for Guy and Duane, but Christmas morning always found gifts for all spread on the dining-room table. Only when Helen was a teenager did they break down and have a Christmas tree.

203

He couldn't help thinking, either, of the bittersweet Christmas season of the year before, when Helen was so close to death. This year he was no longer the recipient of sympathetic glances and careful queries about how everything was in his family, for which he was thankful; at the Home they all lived with one foot in the grave and seldom a month went by but what someone was not taken away by the wagon from the funeral home.

He was reminded of this once more when James Griffin passed aways peacefully in his sleep the week before Christmas. But it didn't seem right to mourn; Dan had been over to the nursing section to see him only a few days before and the two had talked of James's imminent going. He had been almost eager to go. His wife had been dead for years and since they had been childless there were only a few nieces and nephews to mourn his passing.

The next day Newt suffered a stroke and he, too, had to be moved to the nursing section. And John became almost stone deaf—so with the exception of Mandy Swartzentruber, Dan was alone of their small group of Deer Creek residents. The day after James's funeral Dan came down with a heavy cold which threatened to go down to his weak lungs and the doctor forbade him to as much as set foot out in the cold. So for the first since he had become a resident at the Home he spent Christmas Day there.

Since he could not go out, Vernon and Judy came in to see him. It was rather a bleak day for them, too; Jim was spending the Christmas holidays skiing with his girl friend and her parents in Colorado and Gary was going to join them in the days he had off. Both Vernon and Judy couldn't help thinking of last year when Helen had still been with them but so obviously wouldn't be much longer. They had eaten a lonely Christmas dinner at home and then came to the Home in the afternoon to spend a few hours with Dan.

There were few gifts to exchange. Judy had a new warm robe for him and Vernon gave him a pair of house slippers.

204

Since Dan couldn't go out to shop, he gave Judy a check and told her to buy something special to remember him by.

"I don't need that," Judy said warmly. "I'll never forget you as it is. And I don't need anything special; you're special just on your own."

"Why, bless your heart, child. That's the nicest compliment I've ever had."

He had subscribed to the *National Geographic* for Vernon, along with one for each of his own sons and Jake and Alta. Small checks took care of all of his other ten grandchildren.

The night after Christmas he woke to find that the heavy cold had turned to pneumonia again. There was a burning in the back of his throat and every time he coughed he felt as if he were tearing apart. His last coherent thought was to ring for the night nurse and after that he had only confused flashes of reality.

He was rushed to the city hospital by ambulance, where he was put under oxygen and intensive care for forty-eight hours. Not only was he fighting pneumonia this time but after almost eighty-eight years of trouble-free service his heart was faltering.

With tubes in his nose and an IV needle in his arm he was a pathetic sight to Judy, who came in as soon as she heard about him. He had never been a large man; what he lacked in muscle he had made up in spirit, and now he seemed to have shrunken to the size of a ten-year-old child. She could not keep from weeping, although she did so quietly lest she disturb him. She could only press the hand that didn't have the IV needle and hope he knew that she thought he was a great guy, the best Christian example she had ever known in a man, and that she was rooting for him for all she was worth.

He sensed dimly that she was there but this was one struggle he had to go through alone. But, no, he was not alone, he told himself. Jesus Christ, Victor over death, was living in his heart. In those forty-eight hours he seemed to drift nearer and nearer to that great land beyond. And why not, he cried? So many of his beloved ones were waiting there for him, besides the Lord Jesus Himself. It would be wonderful there—no pain, no tubes or needles, no struggle to keep breathing. Above all, complete freedom of the spirit there would be most wonderful.

But the Lord must not have been quite ready to take him home, because at the end of the forty-eight hours he was put into a private room. And after a refreshing sleep he awoke to see someone else besides the nurse or Judy standing beside the bed.

"Why, Alta!" he said weakly. "It is Alta, isn't it? Or am I dreaming?"

"Shh! Yes, it's me. But don't talk. The nurse said I could look in on you if I didn't let you talk. I just arrived by plane and Judy brought me straight from the airport. I'll just sit here beside you for a few minutes, then Judy will take me out to her place."

He nodded ever so slightly and closed his eyes again. He must have been closer to dying than even he had thought to have her here. He thought of his sons and opened his eyes again and looked at Alta.

"Duane and Guy?" He barely mouthed the words.

"They're coming in tonight sometime."

"Jake?"

"He isn't very well. The doctor told him he'd better not come. So I came alone."

He closed his eyes again. She reached down and pressed his hand and sat down beside his bed. If Judy was also in the room he did not sense it. He felt too weak to think and then drifted off to sleep again.

¤   ¤   ¤

He was in the hospital another week and then moved into the nursing section at the Home for three more weeks before he was pronounced well enough to go back to his own room again. After a few days with their father, Duane and Guy left again, Guy because his school was ready to start after Christmas vacation and Duane because his real-estate business in Kansas was so involved he felt he couldn't be away.

Only Alta stayed for the full month until he was back in his room, and she came in to see him every day, sometimes with Judy but just as often without. After he was well enough to talk he began to take a keen delight in her visits. Although they talked some about current events in the world and the church, they shared more often reminiscences of the time when she was still at home, before she left for college. Funny, he thought once wryly, that his thoughts now would be so much in the past when he had been so close to the Great Future only a few weeks before.

Alta wanted to know about the early days of the community and once again he told her of the two families and one single man who had moved in from Ohio and who had come in the spring of 1846 to take up land in the Deer Creek area, Daniel P. Guengerich and family, William Wertz and family, and Daniel's half-brother, Joseph Swartzentruber. He had read about them often and remembered hearing his grandmother Guengerich tell how the struggling little group would have moved away if they'd have had the means to do so, of how Daniel P. had grown discouraged with the thought of all the trees to be cleared from his tract along Deer Creek before he could hope to have a productive farm and had moved to the more open land in Lapland after a few years, of how the first public religious service had been funeral services for one of Daniel P.'s small children, how the first Sunday service was not held until three years after the few families had come to Iowa, and how, with the addition of more families, the first small church was organized in 1851.

"And now there are what, a dozen of them?" Alta asked.

"Probably so, counting the Old Order."

"You mean you count them in on it, too?" she asked.

"Alta, we were all one at the beginning. We all called ourselves Amish Mennonites. We were Amish. There was no calling ourselves Old Order or Mennonite or Conservative Mennonite or what have you. Oh, we had lots of bickering and disagreements among us but up until about 1890 we still all worked together. We were Amish," he repeated again.

"What happened? You're not now. Why, it would insult some people now if you told them that."

"I know. But they can't deny their heritage. You asked what happened—all I can say is we were human. Some were honest differences of conviction and, I'm sorry to say, some were personality clashes. I'm afraid every church split finds its root in that. Maybe our leaders didn't emphasize God's Word enough; maybe too much emphasis was given to human ideas. Of course, the way my convictions lie, I'd say that was the worst fault of the Sharon churches. Too much weight was given to outward form and not enough to the inner life."

"Well, sometimes I think that's reversed among Mennonites now. Or, more correctly, they ignore both and then they don't know where to stop. In our affluent age—"

All at once he was tired, tired not only physically but mentally and emotionally—tired of making endless decisions, of weighing Scriptures, and choosing the way that seemed best out of the endless maze of public opinion and contemporary thought and human opposition. How often through the years had he pondered and prayed and struggled to make the decision that would glorify God and not run counter to his convictions!

Alta must have sensed his mood because she changed the subject and a few minutes later she left him for the day. He walked to the elevator with her, then slowly went back to his room. One of these days he would do that for the last time, he thought.

19

He was sitting in a chair in front of his desk and bookcase contemplating the material before him. Ever since his siege of pneumonia three months ago he felt the need of sorting all books and magazines and letters and papers he had accumulated since he had taken up residence in the Home. One more spell like that and he would go; not that he cared, in fact he was in a mood of expectation about it, but he felt guilty about hugging these things to him and then leaving the disposal of it to Judy and Alta when he was gone.

He had thought he'd given away all of the things that were worthwhile when he moved in here, and truly he had given away some things to the historical society or asked Helen to store some in her attic, besides selling a lot of it at his household auction. But he had kept a few of his most treasured books and pamphlets besides all that had accumulated since then. Savilla used to call him a regular squirrel, and she was impatient with this weakness of his.

He opened the bottom drawer of his desk. Fannie May had just finished cleaning his room so he guessed it was safe to lay things out and sort them into piles. Judy was coming this afternoon and would take some of the things down to the Historical Building, the rest would either be thrown away or join the other keepsakes in Helen's—now Judy's—attic.

There were letters of all kinds in the drawer. Here again Savilla would call him a squirrel, he thought as he picked up a handful. He believed he had kept every one the children had ever written him since he had come here. He dropped them on the desk top and shuffled through them. Mostly, they were letters of the past year or two and he drew one out of the envelope. One from Guy. And here was one from Duane—just a short note scribbled on his office paper in large scrawling letters. He picked up a letter from Guy and several from Alta and Jake. These could all go in a box and be stored in Helen's attic.

In the bottom drawer of the other side of the kneehole desk were all of the cards he had gotten since he came, packed in as tightly as he could manage—birthday cards, sympathy cards at Helen's death, get-well cards for the two times he had had pneumonia, and he knew that if he dug way down to the bottom he would find some of the sympathy cards that had come when Savilla died.

He had already made several piles on his desk and one on the floor when he heard steps outside the door. He looked up just as Fannie May pushed open the half-closed door and came in.

"Why, Dan, what are you doing?" She giggled. "I thought I cleaned your room. Do you want me to come in and do it over again?"

"Not today, I don't. I thought you were done or I wouldn't have started this. Did you forget something?"

"The window cleaner." She looked around and saw it on the dresser where she had used it to clean the mirror. She walked over and picked it up and came and sat on a chair. "What are you doing anyhow?"

"I'm sorting my papers and books and stuff. I don't want to leave this for the poor children to do when I'm gone; so much of it is junk and of no interest to anyone else."

"My, you've got an awful lot of letters. You must write to a lot of people."

"Just the family. Oh, and those are the cards I've received from friends and relatives ever since I've been here, except some sympathy cards I got when Savilla died."

"You must know an awful lot of people. That drawer is packed as full—"

"Yes, it is. But then I guess you can't live in a community as long as I have and not know a lot. Besides, I'm related to most of them."

"Really?"

"Yes, through old Daniel P. Guengerich on Savilla's side, and Daniel J. Gingerich on my side. One was an uncle to the other and they both had large families. They've intermarried along with the Shetlers and Millers and Swartzentrubers until we're a regular Duke's mixture around here. It's a good thing people like your parents came in and brought some new blood. Our community needs it."

She giggled again. "I'm not going to get married so what good does my new blood do?"

"Oh, you might one of these days. You might find a widower and get the job of raising his ten children."

This brought a spell of giggles. "Oh, Dan, you're funny," she gasped, wiping her eyes with a corner of her apron. "But I don't see any widowers in our church with or without children."

"Hmm. Say, how are you getting along in that church?"

She sobered. He knew she had left the Old Order. If one were familiar with the varying degrees of progressiveness one could tell what church a woman belonged to by the way she dressed and already Fannie May had changed some-

211

what. Her covering, for instance, was no longer the organdy the Old Order used but rather the nylon net used by more progressive congregations. And she wore a long coat to work, rather than the short one that was not to be worn without a shawl on top, but few girls did unless they went to church. And the black bonnet of the Old Order women had given way to a scarf tied over her covering, or if it was warm enough, nothing.

"We're going to be taken up by our new church next Sunday," she said.

"Oh, you mean you still aren't?"

"No. But I like it. And Anna Sue likes the young people."

"So? That's good. Does your mother seem contented with it?"

"Oh, she wishes it wouldn't have had to be. But she likes going away in the car this winter when it's cold."

"I bet she does. Who has the car, you or Anna Sue?"

"I bought it but Anna Sue drives it."

"Oh, surely you're going to learn how to drive, too?"

"When it gets warmer I'd like to. After all, Anna Sue won't be around always."

"I was going to say that. Are you going to get a telephone and electricity, too?"

"We can't, Dan. As long as Mama is with the Old Order the preachers would be after her all the time if we got that stuff in the house. It's her house."

"You mean you couldn't install the telephone and pay for it yourself?"

"I don't know. Maybe we will sometime, but not now. I'd feel sorry for Mama if we did—For what they'd do to her."

He sighed. So they were still insisting on the outward form without regard to the inner faith.

"Don't they ever preach salvation through faith in what Christ did for us on the cross?"

"Oh—I'm not saying that some of them don't," she said,

212

absently shaking the bottle of window cleaner in her hand. "Of course, ever since I talked with you—last year when you asked me about a personal commitment to Jesus Christ—ever since then I've noticed those things more. Maybe there really are more of them than I thought. But those seem to be the quiet ones and the ones who think the *Audnung* is more important run the church."

He sighed. He thought of his cousin Christ. He and others like him must have taught their convictions well.

"But I really like the church where I'm going now," Fannie May bubbled. "The people are so friendly and helpful. And I like my Sunday school class. There's a lot of us— single blessings—" She giggled again. "And we get together and have parties and gift exchanges at Christmas—"

"Good. Do you ever have a Bible study, too?"

"So far we haven't. But we have such an interesting Sunday school class! I can't tell you how interesting! You don't know how much it means to be able to ask questions about our lesson and maybe tell what a Bible verse means to me. I love it!"

"I'm glad for you. Keep on studying the Bible and asking questions. It's the way to learn."

"I'm going to."

"Did you find your window cleaner?" He felt mean to remind her about her job but his conscience would not let him keep her in here talking on the Home's time.

She took the hint and got up. "Yes. I'll have to get back to my cleaning. Now don't you make too big a mess in here for me to clean up."

"I'll try not to."

He gave another deep sigh, after she left, when he thought of the Old Order. What basis did they have for their insistence on outward appearance when God said over and over again that the heart of man was the source of his trouble? "For out of the heart proceed evil thoughts, murders, adulteries, fornications, thefts, false witness, blasphemies," Jesus Christ had told the Pharisees. To be sure, when one has the Lord Jesus in the heart He will manifest Himself in the behavior of the person He indwells in such things as meekness, goodness, kindness to others, holy living, a hatred of evil, and a desire to please and honor and glorify God above all else. Dan prayed a silent prayer for their enlightenment as he resumed his sorting.

By the time the dinner bell rang at noon he had sorted out the children's letters he wanted to keep and slipped a rubber band around them, and stuffed the wastebasket full of what he didn't want to keep. He got up stiffly from his chair and reached for his cane; he should never have made that comparison between Newt and a worm since he was getting to be almost as bad. But by the time he reached the elevator the stiffness had eased and he could walk without his cane.

Since the death of James Griffin and Newt's removal to the nursing section two newer residents had been seated at his table. He greeted them along with Mandy and Orpha Bender, another longtime resident, and took his place among the general babble. They all bowed their heads as the administrator asked the blessing and as soon as that was over the chatter began again.

One of the new tablemates, Sam Yoder, began to talk about a grandson. "Why, I don't know what that boy would do if we had another Depression. He's got everything. Everything! Three blue silos, a big dairy barn, three tractors, one big four-wheeler, a four-wheel drive pickup, CB's in his car and pickup, besides all the fancy gadgets in his house you can think of. And now his wife isn't satisfied with the house and they're talking of building a new one. And if I know her it'll have to be a big hundred-thousand-dollar one or she won't even look at it."

"They're all that way," Lewis Byler, the other new tablemate said. "They don't know where to quit. I've got a

214

son like that. He bought a snowmobile just for the fun of it last year and a three-wheeler for his twelve-year-old boy this year. He draws twenty thousand a year and can barely make ends meet. Last year he borrowed money from me to pay the interest on his seventy-five-thousand-dollar house."

"Yes, one of my granddaughers said her husband was looking for another job where he could get more money. He makes six hundred and fifty a month and she says they can't live on it. And they only have two small children. She's even working part time," Orpha Bender said.

"Why must they have so much?" Lewis asked. "We didn't have two or three color TV's and two cars and a pickup and a boat and a lakeside lot and we got along. Bet we were happier, too."

"It's this young generation," Sam said. "I don't know what's wrong with them. All the stuff to buy and people breaking their necks to keep up with the Joneses. I tell you! And at the same time the church giving has fallen off. Why, I was on the mission board for the conference until a year ago and the giving was going down every year. But people have the money to spend on material things."

"That's about like our church," Mandy said. "The last year Amos was still living I know of one family that drove around in a Lincoln but for three years straight they couldn't pay their church dues."

"Well, you'd be surprised at some of the people who send their youngsters to IMS and never pay the tuition," Lewis said, whose granddaughter had been the school secretary for a number of years. "People who seem to have plenty of money for other things."

Through all of this Dan had only listened. He thought of Gary, who was ready to repudiate his father's generation for the very reason these oldsters were protesting, the grabbing for materialism. But all of these being complained about were of Gary's generation so it must not be a malaise of just one group.

215

"Yes sir, I really wonder what would happen if they had to go through a Depression like we did," Sam said.

"They'd crack up," Lewis said.

"Oh, surely not," Mandy protested. "I don't believe they all would. Surely some of the younger generation would dig in and learn to do without—"

"They'd have to," Sam said darkly.

"And make it through, just like we did. Surely some of them have enough faith in God," Mandy finished.

"Sometimes I wonder," Sam said.

Seated beside Dan, Lewis turned, fork in midair and asked, "Dan, you've been sitting here taking this all in; what do you think? What would happen if another Depression hit them like in the thirties?"

"Well, I'm no prophet. But I should hope that Mandy's right. After all, we came through, and I believe our faith in God was stronger for it. At least, I know mine was."

"Yes, but I think we had more to begin with," Sam protested. "I mean faith. We didn't have all of this materialism to distract us. Maybe we were just too stupid and naive to know better but it seems to me that the church meant a lot more to us, oh—say forty—fifty years ago."

"I do, too," Orpha said. "Why, we never dreamed of missing services unless we were too sick to go and nowadays we have grandchildren who go only if they don't have anything else planned."

"Mennonites?" Mandy asked.

"Of course."

Naturally, they didn't get anything settled; one never did at such discussions, Dan thought as they left the dining room afterward. They didn't even expect to when it came right down to it; all they wanted to do was let off steam about the younger generation. Where had he read about that old Greek philosopher who had complained of the decadence of the younger generation over two thousand years ago? Well, things hadn't changed, he thought; young people were still on their way to the dogs and old people were still complaining about it.

He sat in the lounge and watched the noon cartoons for a while and then decided to go back to his room and work again. But he wasn't in the mood for working on the letters again, especially that drawer full of cards, with so many of them from friends at Helen's death. He opened another drawer and shuffled through the contents. Away in the back he came on a bound booklet that he had not seen or thought of in years—he had even forgotten he had it.

Amish and Mennonite Church, Centennial Anniversary, he read the title. There was a picture of East Union on the outside—it had grown considerably from the small group that met in a schoolhouse and for years was called the Werey Church. He leafed through the pages and saw that it was a compilation of all of the sermons and addresses given at the one hundredth birthday of the organization of the church.

He got no more sorting done that day. He began to read and was lost to all that went on around him. He remembered now having attended the all-day celebration but he would not have remembered the speakers or what they said. Much of what was in the booklet he already knew, especially if it was historical in content. There was an address on the beginning of the Mennonite denomination in Switzerland by J. C. Wenger and he read it again with interest even if he had known most of the facts. There was another article by H. S. Bender on the Mennonite concept of the church. He couldn't help thinking that even some of the leaders of the church today, especially the young ones, had deviated from the concept of a brotherhood that had the right to discipline members or to penalize them by withholding fellowship.

The back half of the book was a history of the later developments of the area churches by Guy F. Hershberger and he began to read in that. Time passed quickly as he

217

read but he was oblivious to it, even if the old clock struck three, then four, with half hour strikes between.

And what was this? He came upon part of an article by Daniel Kauffman, written in 1896 and published in the old *Herald of Truth* and quoted by Hershberger, in which Kauffman was reporting on the condition of the churches in this very area. In the past, Kauffman said, the brethren in this area had held too rigidly to old customs, while at the same time not receiving enough indoctrination in the fundamental principles of the gospel. Traditions of men were more emphasized than reading of the Word. New customs and practices were forbidden without regard to their relation to the gospel and as the people came to see that the old rules had no Scripture to support them they tended to regard all restrictions as of men, until the principle of self-denial was lost sight of. And they lost their governor, Dan added in his own thoughts.

He laid down the book and thought over what he had read in the light of what Fannie May had said in the morning and the dinner table conversation at noon. Somewhere between the two extremes was a sensible path for the child of God to follow, he thought. "Dear Lord, this is what we need in this community." He picked up the book and began reading the next paragraph.

"What is the remedy?" Hershberger quoted Kauffman as asking. Ah, here was the answer. Preach the Word! He read on until the last paragraph of the quote when a phrase leapt out at him—"one whose faith and practice is neither formal nor formless."

Neither formal nor formless. He laid down the booklet and leaned across the desk and buried his head in his arms. "Ah, my dear people," he thought, "my dear, dear people." He wished he could get on a high place and shout it out. "You need a faith that is neither formal nor formless. Look, Old Order, if you insist on the outward appearance to the exclusion of the inner heart you end up with an empty husk," he cried silently in his heart. "And you younger people of our church, unless you have Christ in your heart to control your attitudes and your way of life your faith is a formless blah." He began shaking with sobs. "Oh, my people, my people," he cried, "turn back, turn back, not to formalism again, but to the Word of God, to a personal commitment to the Lord Jesus Christ. If that's the faith of our fathers, well and good, but unless that faith is firmly centered on the Christ who died on the cross for the sins of the world, that faith is worthless," he cried silently. No wonder Gary turned from that empty formlessness, but on the other hand, neither could he blame Fannie May for seeking more than formalism.

He shook with sobs until he could cry no more. It seemed to him that his very soul was poured out before the Lord for the sake of his people. Almost he could say with Moses, when he pleaded for the children of Israel in the wilderness, "Yet now, if thou wilt forgive their sin—; and if not, blot me, I pray thee, out of thy book—"

How could one emphasize this clearly enough? He got up and went to the window and watched the cars speed up and down the highway. How could one reach each new generation with the gospel of Jesus Christ and teach them, like the Bible said, to deny ungodliness and worldly lusts—keeping up with the Joneses—if you please, he thought, and live soberly, righteously, and godly in this present world?

He thanked the Lord for young people like Judy, but not only for her, but for all of those dear people of all generations in this area who honestly wanted the Lord in their hearts, for those who sincerely wanted to proclaim the gospel of salvation through faith in His sacrifice on the cross and live their lives in a way that would glorify Him. There were many, he knew. And yet, he thought once more of those who were lost in either formalism or formlessness and the burden pressed down again.

He was an old man and had only a tiny span on this earth

anymore. Whether for good or evil, his witness was almost over. "But, oh, dear Lord," he prayed, "don't ever let this community be without pulpits that proclaim Thy Word. Don't ever let those first brave settlers be without descendants in this community who honestly love Thee and seek to serve Thee. I can die content if I know this to be so."

A meadowlark's song rang clearly through the closed window and he straightened up and rubbed his arm across his eyes, for all the world as he had when he was three years old and Ma had paddled him for some misdemeanor.

A verse of Scripture came to mind. "Jesus Christ, the same yesterday, and to day, and for ever." How appropriate, he thought. Yesterday—for those first struggling settlers who had come so long ago—today—for him and all of those living in the thick of life right now—forever or tomorrow—for Judy and all of her generation and younger ones who were about ready to take over the reins and go on from here. Jesus Christ must be the center pivot of all generations or humanity groped in darkness and loneliness, estranged from the only true source of light, he thought.

Yes, God was good. "I have been young and am now old," he thought, "and I have never seen the righteous forsaken nor his children begging bread."

The supper bell rang. He turned from the window and reached for his cane. "Even so, come quickly, Lord Jesus," he thought. "I'm ready to go."

Clara Bernice Miller, the fifth of ten children, was born into an Amish home in Iowa. Her father left the Amish Church and after years of spiritual wandering joined the Mennonite Church.

Clara was brought up in the Amish tradition. As a child she discovered books and read everything that her father and the school library could put into her hands. Her mother often spanked her because with her nose in a book she neglected household chores. Although this was an unpleasant experience, she now says that it taught her good sense and proper values in life. In her reading she dreamed of becoming a writer.

Her preparation for writing included severe spiritual discipline. She joined the Amish Church at sixteen and married an Amish boy at nineteen. She became the mother of ten children.

Clara and her husband, Wayne, came to wrestle desperately with the meaning of their faith. Mr. Miller suffered illness and they lost one child. Through these experiences God led them finally to a simple, satisfying faith. The Millers are members of the Des Moines Mennonite Church, Des Moines, Iowa.

She is author of *The Crying Heart, Katie,* and *The Tender Herb.*